EMPOWERMENT
AS
CEREMONY

EMPOWERMENT
AS
CEREMONY

WILLIAM M. EPSTEIN

Routledge
Taylor & Francis Group

LONDON AND NEW YORK

First published 2013 by Transaction Publishers

2 Park Square, Milton Park, Abingdon, Oxfordshire OX14 4RN
711 Third Avenue, New York, NY 10017

Routledge is an imprint of the Taylor & Francis Group, an informa business

First issued in paperback 2017

Library of Congress Catalog Number: 2012031236

Library of Congress Cataloging-in-Publication Data

Epstein, William M., 1944-
  Empowerment as ceremony / William M. Epstein.
    p. cm.
  Includes bibliographical references.
  ISBN 978-1-4128-5160-2
  1. Power (Social sciences) I. Title.
  HN49.P6E67 2013
  303.3—dc23

                                                    2012031236

ISBN 13: 978-1-4128-5160-2 (hbk)
ISBN 13: 978-1-138-50954-2 (pbk)

How sharper than a serpent's tooth it is
To have a thankless child
—William Shakespeare, *King Lear*, Act I, Scene IV

Contents

Preface

The social problems of the United States are embedded in its culture. The problems are not technical and neither social services nor economic growth, even with the sanction of social science theory, will resolve them. In fact, the nation's problems have persisted through decades of social welfare provision and in spite of enormous economic growth. Rather than unfortunate dislocations of a beneficent ethos, the nation's social problems, by and large, are engendered by social preferences that are romantic more than pragmatic. The social services as well as the distribution of economic growth are expressions of these social values. Empowerment practice is a characteristic instance of the pitfalls of American policy romanticism.

Despite its pretenses to radical change, contemporary empowerment practice in the United States is a civic church of national values, clearer in performing its ceremonial role than god-based churches whose day care centers, men's clubs, bible classes, and singles nights obscure their essential civic rituals. Empowerment practice and American social welfare generally embody determinative cultural preferences in the same way that photography, painting, sculpture, and music open windows into deeper social meaning. David Hume might well see it occupying the same role as the Church of England that he claimed received its public subsidies as a "bribe to indolence"—the perverse antithesis of the political activism that empowerment practice claims.[1] By itself, empowerment practice is not worth the effort of an extended commentary, as it achieves none of its program goals and has not even bothered to accumulate a respectable critical literature. However, similar to social welfare and the personal social services, it is a portrait of the society given meaning by its embrace of social values. To understand empowerment practice is to peer deeply into decisive American social values.

Perhaps as professional caution or misconceived loyalty, the small number of evaluations of social welfare practice only delicately trace back to the forces that give a program its essential cultural meaning. The typical critique largely restricts itself to description and rarely addresses effectiveness, let alone the actual social preferences that sustain the program. Nonetheless, the emptiness of empowerment practice as social welfare—the absence of credible evaluations of practice—is the only conclusion that approximates certainty. The virtues of empowerment practice in resolving social deprivations are speculations of hope without evidence. The ambiguities created by inadequate, incomplete, and misleading information are apparently tolerated, if not actually nurtured, by practice and the culture itself.

The paradoxical persistence of empowerment practice—popularity without effectiveness—is resolved by its ceremonial role in affirming basic tenets of American ideology, in particular an exaggerated form of individualism and individual responsibility. More generally, the dominance of a ceremonial role over a true production function in social welfare says much about the pervasive inadequacies of America's social provisions, the weaknesses of the occupations that staff its agencies, and their tepid intellectual presence in the university.

The paradox of persistence recalls the conditions of American preferences, that is, the justifications for American policy choices. These choices explored through empowerment practice constitute a determinative American ideology—democratic populism—that is romantic rather than pragmatic. The continuing investment in empowerment practice defers attention to the deep cultural and economic inequalities of the nation. Happiness has forever been elusive, and existential angst may be inevitable. However, it is probably more agreeable to be miserable in an egalitarian society than in a highly stratified one.

Despite its Enlightenment pretensions, the nation has largely rejected democratic progressivism. Policy romanticism pervades the culture and naturally expresses itself in public policy. Contrary to popular antagonisms toward the public sector, the American government is an obedient creature of its very open society. The antagonisms are legitimate but better focused on the populist dominance of the nation's democracy, its appetite for ignorance, neglect, and cruelty.

The view of American society through the lens of empowerment practice is neither an assault on American society nor a condemnation of its openness. Indeed, it is a tribute to both in the hope that a more decent national ethos emerges from consideration of its faults. Still and all, hope does not constitute much of a program for change.

This book lays out its themes in the introduction but waits until after the long consideration of empowerment practice to develop them in the final chapter. The conclusions of empowerment practice are obvious extensions of the analysis that considers the best of the vast empowerment literature.[2] However, the interpretation of the conclusions are inescapably speculative, as there is no credible research method that produces apodictic evidence of what determines social outcomes. That is, the United States cannot be divided into experimental and control regions in which a series of variables are manipulated over generations in order to discover the causes of social outcomes. This methodological limitation seriously circumscribes the ability of the social sciences to identify true causal elements of social problems and to reach true scientific standing as disciplines.

Nonetheless, the social sciences have accommodated social tastes and carved out decisive social roles for themselves by constantly looking for relatively simple remedies for social problems that are both inexpensive and compatible with contemporary social arrangements. These simple factors—counseling, tutoring, psychotherapy, a bit of day care or job training, and so forth—then become the core justifications for social services. Inevitably, they fail but still they persist. However, they persist as ceremonies of social values rather than as solutions to social problems. Empowerment practice and the social services generally are as much cultural institutions as July 4th parades, Mother's Day, and the Pledge of Allegiance.

Notes

1. A gem of a phrase attributed to David Hume in his friend Adam Smith's *The Wealth of Nations.*
2. More than 13,000 *Social Sciences Citation Index* articles (Thompson Reuters) since 1960, together with an enormous number of books and unindexed material impose a difficult challenge to any review of empowerment practice. A great effort was made to identify the principal, most influential material and to analyze at least a sampling of the best of it, although it was rare to find any study at all that conformed to the expectations for solid empirical research. Frequently cited, prominent works on empowerment (e.g., Solomon 1976; Gutierrez 1990) and their citations in the *Social Sciences Citation Index* were mined for evaluations of empowerment programs. The bibliographies of books on empowerment were similarly searched. In addition to the *Social Sciences Citation Index*, many other databases were searched for evaluations of empowerment programs published after 1995: child development and adolescent studies, family and society studies worldwide, general science collection, health source-nursing/academic edition, masterfile premier, psych articles, psychinfo, socindex, and women's

studies international. Many key terms were searched and combined for all years, among them being *empowerment, empowering, women, feminist, randomized controlled trials, blacks, African Americans, Latinos, Hispanics, Asian, sexual minorities, gay, outcomes, Chinese,* and *evaluation.* Except for rare instances, only domestic programs are included in this analysis.

Introduction

There are many in the United States who are poor, who lead socially marginal lives, and who are in need of jobs as well as basic services such as education, medical care, and housing, among others. There are multitudes in other parts of the world, who in addition to being poor, are also oppressed in the truest and most objective sense of the word: jailed, tortured, and killed for being in the wrong ethnic group or for exercising their conscience and expressing political opinions. Empowerment practice claims an ability to liberate the oppressed largely through self-organization, self-motivation, self-invention, and even "self-clarity."

Empowerment as a goal and a practice, that is, a method to achieve its goal, started out with actual political and social oppression in mind. Yet, over the decades since Freire and Fanon, who continued the radical political tradition, its target and meaning has slowly been vulgarized to include just about any process that increases the capacity of an individual to manipulate his or her environment. In this way, traditional mental health treatment, much of nursing, community organization and development, case management, legal advocacy, psychotherapy, and much else has been reframed as empowerment practice. Yet, the force of empowerment theory and its justification for strong interventions rested with the extreme circumstances of people in need—their political oppression, social marginality, poverty, grave inequalities, and the like. As the concept has become widened in contemporary empowerment practice to include the mundane and trivial, so too has it stretched the conditions of oppression to justify its attention to common situations of need and quietly excuse its near-uniform ineffectiveness. The contemporary practice of empowerment mocks the revolutionary impulse with interventions paraded for review in insurrectionary battle fatigues. Without its camouflage, it is reduced to shameless self-promotion devoid of any respect for skepticism and fact.

1

The popularity of empowerment practice has accelerated enormously since the 1960s,[1] coinciding with its pacification, its vulgarization, and the decline of its novelty. What was initially a theory of release from illegitimate social constraints has become a practice of adaptation to the prevailing social values that endorse social inequalities. Empowerment practice has undercut political and social reform, as its attention has shifted subtly from unjust conditions to personal imperfection. The therapeutic has triumphed, and structural change has yielded to individual adaptation. Still, the vitality of empowerment lies in addressing serious material deprivations and otherwise objective violations of cultural norms—the conditions of substantial inequality that the field has rejected. Nonetheless, planned societal change in behalf of greater equality may, in fact, be impossible; however, the acknowledgment of futility carries more of a revolutionary hope than the perpetuation of hypocrisy.

Although initially a creation of the left, empowerment practice is central to modern social work, the helping professions, and the contemporary American ethos as it addresses the poor, needy, and in other ways economically and social marginal groups. Yet, there is no demonstrably effective practice to fulfill its goals; that is, the effectiveness of professional interventions that are dedicated to empowering weak groups, to liberating the oppressed, and to preserving subcultural integrity has never been demonstrated. The essential tenets of empowerment practice are romantic expressions of democratic populism rather than of pragmatic social progressivism. They perform ceremonial affirmations of extreme individualism and an exaggerated sense of personal responsibility without achieving programmatic goals that benefit those in need or challenging orthodox political priorities.

More troubling than simply an empty series of programmatic misadventures, the empowerment promise to improve the lot of blacks, Hispanics, women, sexual minorities, and others has come to stand for its very opposite: a reactionary tribalism that imposes a voluntary apartheid of special claims to privileged relief on grounds of fictive oppression. Modern empowerment practice—as rhetorically hyperbolic as its inspirations—creates a series of the imaginary oppressed that undermines legitimate claims and marginalizes even further those in need.

Rather than rebelling against the institutionalized values, notably an extreme individualism, that are associated with the worrisome socioeconomic stratification of the United States, the practice of empowerment and indeed the helping professions generally affirms those values. The helping professions may be well intentioned but thwarted by overwhelming constraints, but more likely, they are complicit in the denial of greater equality. Indeed, the practice of liberation is in good Orwellian standing by asserting universal values that it denies in its parochial programs. The programs only benefit a few professionals while preserving the inequalities of contemporary American society.

American society remains remarkably complacent in the face of serious economic threats and disparities. The large American income disparities have grown even larger since 1979 when the twenty-first percentile averaged $15,500 in household income per year after federal taxes and income transfers and the minimum of the ninety-ninth percentile earned a comparable household income of $115,965 (Congressional Budget Office 2011, 37). In 2007, the disparity had grown from $18,979 for the twenty-first percentile to $252,607 for the ninety-ninth. Put another way, the income for the wealthy more than doubled, while the income for the near poor grew by only about one fifth. The share of household income after federal taxes and transfers going to the poor (the lowest quintile of household income) fell from about 8 percent in 1979 to about 5 percent in 2007 (ibid., xiii). Through the same period, the comparable share of total income for the wealthiest 20 percent rose from 43 to 53 percent, while the comparable share for the top 1 percent of households rose from almost 8 percent to 17 percent (ibid., xii). While average federal tax rates as a percentage of household income fell for all income groups during this period, the top 1 percent benefited the most: their overall federal tax rate fell from about 38 percent of household income in 1979 to below 30 percent in 2007 (ibid., 26). Yet, during the same period, the nation grew wealthier—the adjusted gross domestic product rose from $8.5 trillion in 1979 to $15.7 trillion in 2007 ($15.1 trillion in 2010)—and, thus, the United States had a greater capacity to address its inequities. Instead, it grew more unequal (ibid., 11).

More troubling, the nation's growing stratification casts a shadow over its vaunted promise of rewarding hard work that is even larger than its great inequality. Economic mobility in the United States, the core of its claim on exceptionalism, is among the lowest of industrial states (Mazumber 2005; Jantti 2006; Burtless 2007). The rigidity is not simply economic but also a reflection of all the other social institutions,

3

notably education, family, and community, that contribute to economic mobility.

Bertelsmann and Stiftung (2011) measured social justice among the thirty-one nations that comprise the Organization for Economic Co-operation and Development (OECD). In addition to South Korea, Japan, New Zealand, and Australia, the other twenty-one members are, by and large, the most industrialized nations in the west. Only Chile, Mexico, and Turkey suffered greater income inequality than did the United States. Despite enjoying one of the highest per capita incomes in the world and by far the greatest national wealth, the United States ranked at or near the bottom for overall poverty prevention, overall poverty rate, child poverty rate, senior citizen poverty rate, preprimary education, and health. The United States also ranks below the OECD average for intergenerational justice and access to education and only slightly above the average for labor market inclusion, social cohesion, nondiscrimination, and labor market inclusion. The United States failed to shine on even one measure of social justice.

The financial crisis and the recession that began in December 2007 increased American poverty, unemployment, underemployment, and homelessness. Poverty rates climbed to 15.1 percent in 2010, more than a 20 percent increase from 12.3 in 2006 (Bureau of the Census 2010). Homelessness increased to more than 1.5 million individuals by 2010 (US Department of Housing and Urban Development 2011). Moreover, the concentration and isolation of low-income minorities has persisted and perhaps even intensified since 1970, even while the geographic integration of wealthier minorities has increased (Fischer 2003; Iceland 2004).

As reported by the Financial Crisis Inquiry Commission (2011), through 2010 about eight million jobs were lost. Unemployment continued through 2011 to hover around 10 percent, while the number of discouraged and underemployed workers brought the total of the economically distressed to almost twenty-six million by the end of 2010 (ibid., xvi). In 2009, unemployment was 6 percentage points higher for blacks and about 3 percentage points higher for Hispanics (Financial Crisis Inquiry Commission 2011).

Total housing value fell almost one third by early 2009: "of the $17 trillion lost from 2007 to the first quarter of 2009 in household net wealth . . . about $5.6 trillion was due to declining house prices . . ." (Financial Crisis Inquiry Commission 2011, 391). Housing foreclosures displaced millions and decimated home equity (the largest source of

4

wealth, by far, for most families) of many middle-income and poorer homeowners. "When the economic damage finally abates, foreclosures may total between 8 million and more than 13 million. . . ." (402). At the same time, Americans have abided costly military misadventures—pointless in Iraq and feckless in Afghanistan—that have already consumed trillions of dollars. In addition, serious social problems persist in child and adult health, including a pandemic of obesity, substance abuse, and access to health services as well as in areas such as mental health care, education, and criminal justice.

The American economic crisis spread across the world. In reaction, riots took place in Italy, England, and Greece, and large demonstrations occurred in most other European nations to demand greater government action to handle the turmoil of the recession. In the United States, discontent was expressed mostly on the political right with the Tea Party heading up the increasing disaffection of Americans with public recourses. The Occupy movement, never forceful, well organized, articulate, or attractive to those affected by the recession, has descended into a squabble over squatters' rights. Public policy in the United States has refused to extend itself to protect homeownership; to make more than token gestures of support to the unemployed, underemployed, and discouraged workers; or to shift the burden of public support for those in need to wealthier citizens. Its most lavish efforts were made on behalf of the banks and the auto industry, while it still refuses to impose prudent public regulation on the financial industry. The modest economic stimulus package came along with tax cuts and largely benefited more comfortable citizens.

The community of economists in the main endorses Keynes' logic of demand-side stimuli to resolve recessions. However, enduring political opinion sustains Hayek and free markets, ever hopeful that the "spontaneous orders" of unregulated competition will somehow provide a broad financial boon and social institutions that promote freedom and decency (Hamowy 1987; Wapshott 2011).

The nation's conservative preferences—an extreme sense of individualism and personal responsibility that is embedded in a distaste for market regulation—and other mystical components of romantic social policy may explain its long-standing and stolid reluctance to institute tough market regulation or generous social provisions for those in need. Yet, whatever the cause, the reality seems inescapable that the nation calmly accepts its problems with a near religious faith that things will get better through the natural, relatively unfettered processes of market and society. In considering the many needy, the nation assumes that in some form they are complicit in their problems. Indeed, many of the needy make the same assumption, although rarely, about themselves.[2] The United States has an upper class and a middle class, but it lacks a lower class except to the extent to which those classes assign underclass status to the needy.

Empowerment practice is an expression of American complacency that engages in the literary theatrics of liberation. It is an institution of American society, but one without a production function in achieving material ends. It claims to pursue specific goals—political and social liberation of oppressed people—and then to operate programs that are instrumental to those ends. However, empowerment practice has never demonstrated a capacity to achieve social and political change, let alone liberate oppressed people. Similarly, it has never demonstrated either that its clinical forms contribute to liberation or that it has produced any outcome of political and social importance. Its only successes—even these are customarily dubious due to weak research—are achieved by redefining customary improvements in basic human function such as dressing oneself, taking medicine, preparing one's own food, and the like, as empowerment. However, this is empowerment without much social meaning and surely even less political effect.

Empowerment practice fashions itself on the radical tradition, yet it pursues transformations neither of human consciousness nor of its material casket. In actuality, the field is enacting a reactionary tribalism of cultural preservation. It stands for the preservation of imaginary, contrived subcultures rather than vital cultural forms shared by distinct minorities. This ceremonial role is convenient for a complacent America that would rather understand deprivation as a normative subcultural preference than as a structural failure of the society. This is not a process of inclusion, understanding, and civil respect, but one that reinforces prevailing stereotypes. Yet, it is ever so polite and helpful, sincere in the belief that it is liberating the oppressed. Nonetheless, no form of segregated empowerment practice (that is, practice restricted to a particular subculture) can demonstrate unique characteristics of the subgroups that constitute variant cultural patterns. However, this failure of scholarship does not impede the field from simply asserting unique characteristics that justify its segregated approach to liberation. Moreover, the field is uniformly unconscious of the possibility that it is perpetuating through its professional certitude the underlying

American belief that the apparent failure of demographic groups (notably minorities of the poor) is due to their own primitiveness. Moreover, the primitiveness is assumed to be the normal condition of oppositional, poor American minorities that refuse to abide by national expectations. Many members of these groups concur in the assessment and perpetuate their own stereotype.

Ceremony

Sociology and anthropology contain a rich exploration of acknowledged ceremonies. Ceremonies, including rituals and rites as opposed to production functions, have a symbolic meaning but lack a purposive or instrumental value in achieving specific ends. Rather than creating an economic good or pursuing a manifest, intended social end, ceremonies are expressive, signifying specific values. The core assumption that institutionalized ceremonies express widely shared social values underpins the study of ceremonies as a tool to investigate society.

Ceremonies are "a form of social action in which a group's values and identity are publicly demonstrated or enacted in a stylized manner, within the context of a specific occasion or event" (Islam and Zyphur 2012, 115). Crucially, ceremonies are without material content, they are "make-believe," constructed only of symbols whose meaning lies in what they signify rather than in what they contain. Symbolism is far more than simple adornment. As Gusfield notes,

> Symbolic aspects of law and government do not depend on enforcement for their effect. They are symbolic in a sense close to that used in literary analysis. The symbolic act invites consideration rather than overt reaction. There is a dimension of meaning in symbolic behavior which is not given in its immediate and manifest significance but in what the action connotes for the audience that views it. (Gusfield 1963, 176–77)

The car as a production function is a material means of transportation but as a symbol "for the audience that views it," the car confers status, group membership, individual style, and the like. Similarly, psychotherapy as a production function is intended to achieve its goals of assuaging a variety of mental problems such as depression, eating disorders, social adjustment, and so forth; as a ceremony, psychotherapy only expresses a series of values—idealized self-reliance and extreme individualism—that may have little relationship to its own clinical goals.

The classic literature of sociology and anthropology often pair the expressive value of ceremonies to a variety of social and political ends. Ceremonies mark boundaries of acceptable behavior and define deviance in seeking to maintain social solidarity; they reinforce acceptable behavior and stigmatize deviance; they define status and the passage from one social role to another. Even without any intrinsic substance they are important elements in the acculturation to social groups and society itself. Following Gusfield (1963), ceremonies dramatize social values and have political importance in furthering the social standing and goals of specific groups. Taking the example of the temperance movement in the United State, he argued that

> Prohibition and Temperance have operated as symbolic rather than as instrumental goals in American politics. The passage of legislation or the act of public approval of Temperance has been as significant to the activities of the Temperance movement as has the instrumental achievement of an abstinent society. The agitation and struggle of the Temperance adherents has been directed toward the establishment of their norms as marks of social and political superiority. The distinction between political action as significant per se and political action as means to an end is the source of the theory underlying [this] analysis of the Temperance movement. (Gusfield 1963, xxxx)

A bit of Mississippi folk wisdom makes the point with greater charm: many people would vote dry even if they had to stagger to the polls to do so.

Van Gennep (1960) and Turner (1969) concluded that rites of passage are powerful tools of socialization. "[R]ituals, ceremonials, dramas, and latterly films may have sufficient power and plausibility to replace eventually the force-backed political and jural models that control the centers of society's ongoing life" (Turner 1969, vii). In fact, similar to all rites of passage, ceremonies of status reversal—temporary exchanges between the high status and the low status—reinforce social structure.

> In the first, the system of social positions is not challenged. The gaps between the positions, the interstices, are necessary to the structure . . . The structure of the whole equation depends on its negative as well as its positive signs. Thus, humility reinforces a just pride in position, poverty affirms wealth, and penance sustains virility and health. . . . While the structurally well endowed seek release [from the burdens of their responsibilities] structural underlings may well seek . . . deeper involvement in a structure that, though fantastic

and simulacral only, nevertheless enables them to experience for a legitimated while a different kind of a "release" from a different kind of lot. (Turner 1969, 201).

Ceremonies of degradation and social exile may strengthen social cohesiveness by creating the other, the "outsider," as an object of moral scorn (Garfinkel 1956). Garfinkel's insights have been greatly elaborated by Goffman (1962) and Waxman (1977) in elucidating processes of prejudice and discrimination that create the stigma of deviance and the scapegoating of deviants. Garfinkel (1956) pointed to the courts as a principal institutionalized vehicle of degradation.

In our society, the arena of degradation whose product, the redefined person, enjoys the widest transferability between groups has been rationalized, at least as to the institutional measures for carrying it out. The court and its officers have something like a fair monopoly over such ceremonies, and there they have become an occupational routine. (Garfinkel 1956, 424).

The mirror image, the ceremony of status elevation, praise, and inclusion, may work a reverse process that welcomes the sinner into the fold of the chosen and the renegade back into the graces of customary society. Following Turner, the elevation of status may be achieved through a variety of "liminal" experiences in which the higher status is conferred through a period of retreat and perhaps even ordeals of self-discovery (Turner 1969).

Ceremonies are acts of cultural persistence and expressions of tradition that contribute to social order (Shils 1971). Ceremonies are "mechanisms which connect the various cross-sections or states of belief at a series of points in time" (Shils 1971, 124).[3] Ceremonies transmit social values between generations and among social groups and within the context of their tradition, they signify legitimacy. A rite of passage legitimizes a person in a new role and sustains tradition.

The classic literature of ceremony is largely concerned with social activities that are acknowledged to be ceremonial. There is no literature of the crypto-ceremonial, that is, social arrangements that pretend to be instrument but persist for their ceremonial role. However, the study of ceremonies has explored symbolic roles within instrumental organizations and social institutions. The exploration of ceremonies within productive organizations has argued that acts that express organizational values can have substantial influence over productivity.

Meyer and Rowan's (1977) seminal typology of organizations facilitated the study of ceremonies in complex organizations. They

9

suggested that complex organizations fall along a continuum which runs from the purely instrumental to the purely ceremonial. Yet, production functions and ceremonial functions may actually be independent characteristics of organizations that can, for example, have both high ceremonial meaning and high productive value. This would seem to be the goal of much commercial advertising that seeks to pair the products with cherished social values in order to increase their market share; for example, Budweiser's red, white, and blue labels and their identification with traditional symbols of American patriotism. In contrast, organizations that have neither a production function nor a ceremonial value perish.

In their comprehensive reviews of ceremony in complex organizations, Trice and Beyer (1984), largely building on Gusfield (1963) and Turner (1969), consolidate a definition of ceremony that is germane to empowerment practice: ceremonies are often repeated social dramas and ritual metaphors—that is, symbolic activities without apparent production functions—that are planned, relatively elaborate, have social consequences, and are addressed to specific audiences. They are expressive even while they are often associated with a variety of social purposes; for example, recognition of changed status, boundary maintenance, cultural solidarity, and so forth (655). Trice and Beyer (1984) are clear that ceremony enhances production through "the ceremonial requirements of managerial roles." In a later, similar review, Islam and Zyphur (2012) reach similar conclusions: "that cognitive or affective processes cause such outcomes as organizational identification or commitment might be complemented by a perspective that views such outcomes as mediated by sense making events or enactments by social groups" (133). Yet, these findings tend to convert the ceremonial into the instrumental; symbolic gestures seem to have material consequences.

Empowerment practice is ceremonial to the extent to which it lacks an immediate production function, in which case it would seem to perform as a social drama that serves to express social values. Without the ability to achieve its goals, empowerment practice becomes ritual—"a standardized, detailed set of techniques and behaviors that manage anxieties, but seldom produce intended, technical consequence of practical importance" (Trice and Beyer 1984, 655). The interventions of empowerment practice—its detailed set of techniques—do not produce empowerment but the elements of ceremony similar to psychotherapy: following Turner (1969), a "liminal" experience in transition from one status to another. In this sense of ceremony, the purpose of empowerment practice is to symbolize the elevated status of the relatively powerless. However, without actually conferring greater power, this ritualized transition acts on behalf of the broader culture's insistence on self-reliance rather than on behalf of the redistributive goals of empowerment practice. Indeed, the perpetuation of empowerment practice—typically funded by public money—would appear politically anomalous if the very institution that it attempted to revolutionize were the source of its sanction. Neither the classic literature of ceremonies nor application to complex organizations seems to offer any example of a reputedly instrumental activity that exists only for its ceremonial value. When not specifically addressing acknowledged ceremonies, the typical inquiry looks at the ceremonial aspects of social institutions and activities.

There are numerous examples of social arrangements, notably social welfare programs whose principal role is performed as a ceremony of social values rather than as a vehicle of social welfare. Indeed, social work has often been criticized over its many years for ceremonializing dominant social values rather than providing material sustenance, achieving the remission of deviance, or offering effective advocacy on behalf of the needy. The same criticism has often been extended more generally to American social welfare. In spite of the nation's wealth, it refuses to remedy poverty or the great inequities of the market, but rather performs rituals of degradation (eg, the stigma of poverty attached to the receipt of welfare). Moreover, the minimal, inadequate material benefits of public programs for the poor (e.g., the Earned Income Tax Credit, Temporary Assistance for Needy Families, Supplemental Security Income, food programs, and others) affirm the deeply held American value of extreme individualism, the assumption that the poor should be more self-reliant. In fact, taken together, combined public benefits rarely reach even the low standard of the American poverty line for the most deserving citizens; for example, dependent children and the totally and permanently disabled. Yet, unlike empowerment practice, the weakest public social welfare arrangements provide some material benefit. In a sense, empowerment practice is a tribute to the endurance and strength of pure ceremony, an observation that underscores the parallel force of the expressive arts—literature, music, and the like.

Empowerment practice would seem to be a poor candidate for the study of ceremony. It looks similar to a typical personal social service that offers methods for enhancing personal performance, social standing, and political efficacy. Yet, the analysis of its literature turns up no credible, systematic, objective evidence that it has achieved any of its goals. Empowerment practice as ceremony offers an explanation for its persistence and perhaps a step toward the resolution of a basic difficulty in the literature of ceremonial functions: the isolation of cause.

Empowerment practice is generally acknowledged to be an instrumental enterprise, not a ceremony, but yet it has no demonstrable production function. Indeed, if ceremony is defined residually as what remains after all instrumental meaning is eliminated, then empowerment practice would qualify as the quintessential ceremony. If it does not persist as a ceremony of cultural values, then it would offer the most curious situation of a complex social institution that endures and even grows more popular without any apparent function. Aside from a role as ceremony, there does not appear to be an alternative explanation.[4]

An enduring ambiguity challenges the various definitions of ceremony. On the one hand, the different definitions customarily agree that ceremonies are symbolic and empty of production functions. On the other hand, ceremonies are consistently tied to a variety of social effects—boundary maintenance, recognition of status, labeling, and so forth—that are assumed to have social consequences (eg, hierarchy and socialization). Yet, these effects are not considered production functions even while social coherence and social order would seem to be essential requirements for the continuation of any society. For example, "the efficacy of traditional healing ceremonies, especially for individuals whose conditions are the result of compound trauma" (Domina 2004, xii) has been often asserted by psychiatrists and psychotherapists through shaman activities (Frank 1973), placebo effects (Moloney, forthcoming), and metaphors (Combs and Freedman 1990). Credibly documented placebo effects would seem to suggest a production function for ceremonies in clinical healing.

The problem of distinguishing symbolic meaning from instrumental, utilitarian, or material meaning is shifted but not resolved by defining the differences as "manifest meanings that are immediately apparent and latent meanings, [that are] not immediately apparent but perceptible" (Gusfield and Michalowicz 1984, 419). However, levels of meaning are not more amenable to clarity, objective demonstration, or use as variables in coherent research. They also lend themselves to more literary analyses of meaning although not necessarily testable statements of how symbolism translates into action, that is, the role of symbolism as the cause or the effect of a variety of social phenomena. The problem of disentangling symbolism from the utilitarian or instrumental is perhaps simplified when the object of study has only a symbolic meaning.

Empowerment practice does not seem to persist for any direct, demonstrable clinical, social, or political function but rather purely for its symbolism, which, in turn, may serve certain diffuse social ends of simply ratifying social values. That is, empowerment practice has no manifest function, only a latent function. Yet, this ratification is probably not empty, but has an eventual material effect. The problem remains to credibly demonstrate the causal relationship between ceremony and its social and material effects. Moreover, if the disciplines that concern themselves with ceremony are to achieve their standing as mature sciences, then the demonstration needs to apply scientifically credible methods.

In the end, the distinction between economic production and social function, that is, between material and symbolic, may not be as important as the causal effects of either. The pairings of ceremonies with consequences are, in essence, causative statements that argue that ceremonies create specific consequences or are the effects of other causes. However, the research cannot employ experimental designs that are recognized as the definitive methods for establishing cause; existent social arrangements are not amenable to randomization. Typically, the literature relies on participant observation and usually for a relatively short period of time. This opens the conclusions to numerous alternative explanations relating to the biases and ignorance of the researchers, the idiographic nature of the experience, and so forth. In short, the precursors and consequences of expressive functions in field research are at best only weakly established. To describe a ceremony is not the equivalent of describing its meaning. The study of irrationality does not require irrational methods.

Even without the ability to make strong statements of relationship let alone cause, the literature of social ceremony, and notably its classic expression, is richly descriptive and intellectually provocative. Even as disciplined speculation, it raises important questions about social meaning, not least of which is skepticism both to rationality in social decision making and to the exceptionalism of the American experience—the presumption that it is a light unto human civilization. The cultural forms that address primal human needs for food, clothing, shelter, and procreation and secondary desires for entertainment and sociability are not necessarily written into the human genome. The attributes of culture are not easily predictable, and human social variation may be far more a ceremonial function than an extension of human rationality. Turner recognized the social indeterminacy of ceremony even while it is typically associated with processes of socialization intended to reproduce abiding conformity and social continuity.

> Through ceremonial processes and social processes more generally, the possibility exists of standing aside not only from one's own social position but from all social positions and of formulating a potentially unlimited series of alternative social arrangements. That this danger is recognized in all tolerably orderly societies is made evident by the proliferation of taboos that hedge in and constrain those on whom the normative structure loses its grip during such potent transitions as extended initiation rites in "tribal" societies and by legislation against those who in industrial societies utilize such . . . genres as literature, the film and the higher journalism to subvert the axioms and standards of the *ancient regime.* . . . (Turner 1969, 13–14).

The Enlightenment inspiration that impelled both sociology and anthropology to study social phenomena is tied to the assumption that understanding would lead to progress in civilization. Both disciplines, even without the use of definitive science and in spite of the intrusive politicalization of scholarship (Horowitz 1993), have challenged the ethnocentrism and provincialism that blemish modern society. However, empowerment practice defies this tradition. Its literature is an instance of factional politics subverting social science scholarship, while its ceremonial drama symbolizes a step backward from the pursuit of a decent common culture toward tribal parochialism.

Notes

1. A keyword ("topic") search in Thomson Reuter's Social Sciences Citation Index for *empowerment* and *empowering* produced the following 13,058 unduplicated hits between 1960 and October 2011. The "topic" search covers titles, abstracts, and author key words. Articles accounted for approximately 85 percent of the hits; the remainder included books reviews, proceeding papers, editorial material, and others. Between 1960 and 1969, there was only one hit; between 1970 and 1984, 48 hits, about 3.2 per year; between 1985 and 1999, 3,383 hits, about 227.5 per year; and between 2000 and 2011, 9,346 hits, about 849.7 per year. The hits appeared across a great number of fields, in descending order of occurrence: public, environmental, and occupational health; nursing; social work; education

and educational research; the management DISCIPLINESs; and scores of additional fields.

2.   American attitudes to the provision of welfare in its narrow sense of programs for the poor have been remarkably consistent and negative across more than sixty-five years of polling, which may also go far to explain the inadequacy of public welfare. See, as examples, Epstein (2004, 2010); Patterson (2000); and Burt and Nightingale (2010).

3.   As such, they would seem to challenge Shils' (1971) criticism that the social sciences are too concerned with the present. After all, cultural anthropology seems obsessed with tradition.

4.   The public's specific ignorance of the failure of empowerment practice—and thus its continuation out of inertia—is not a plausible alternative explanation. The widespread ignorance of most social conditions is not the equivalent of social ignorance. The society, through the multitude of its organizations, has a detailed awareness of social reality. These organizations act in a variety of roles citizens sanction through their participation in society, that is, their daily choices of role that endorse organizations that exist to promote those roles. The awareness of social detail generally restricted to the competitive role of organizations implies neither the manipulation of social preferences by hidden forces nor their illegitimate control of social decision making. Rather, the process of informed decision making even when restricted to elite decision makers is still consensual in an open society. See Epstein (2010) for a detailed exploration of the ecology of role organizations.

Empowerment Practice

Freire and Fanon: The Radical Template
of Empowerment Theory

In counterpoint to pacifist tactics of noncooperation, Freire and Fanon were articulate voices of the violent political tradition that encompassed the revolutions of the left during the twentieth century. In appreciation of violent mass mobilization and nationalism, they also recall the radicalism of the Fascists. Fanon sought the liberation of the colonized from their European oppressors by mobilizing the masses, largely the peasantry, glorifying a violence that was both politically and psychologically empowering. He initially advocated racial and ethnic solidarity and a national consciousness to facilitate wars against colonial oppressors, usually European nations, but then generalized violent insurrection of oppressed groups in developed nations, notably that of blacks in the United States (Fanon 1952, 1965).

Fanon was wrong on almost every note of optimism for a nurturing decency emerging from the successful nationalist movements that displaced colonial governments. The remarkable victory of Mandela and the African National Congress occurred, by and large, without violent conflict between the oppressed and the oppressor. Something other than the "violence of the colonized" united black South Africans. Furthermore, a multiethnic nation becoming homogeneous was beyond his temper and imagination.

Yet, Fanon's appetite for violence did not work out in much of liberated Africa. He claimed that

> Violence in its practice is totalizing and national . . . it harbors in its depths the elimination of regionalism and tribalism. . . . At the individual level violence is a cleansing force. It rids the colonized of their inferiority complex, of their passive and despairing attitude. (Fanon 1963, 51)

17

In fact, the initial postcolonial regimes were frequently repressive, in part, to quiet regionalism and tribalism that emerged in full violent flower once again when the colonial oppressors were themselves removed. Few postcolonial nations in the latter twentieth century have avoided the internal repressions of their liberating regimes—Iraq, Iran, Rwanda, Uganda, Nigeria, and Zimbabwe as examples. They often reprised the same antidemocratic practices as the colonial oppressors and usually without the luxurious Marxian excuses of imposing the will of the masses through a program of reeducation, but rather with the common claim that security was necessary for development. The wretched of the earth are still wretched in spite of the radical political successes of anticolonial armed revolutions.

Indeed, if genocide and mass murder measure the bestial in society, then postcolonialism is not much of an improvement over colonialism, witness Rwanda, Cambodia, the Cultural Revolution in China, partition in India, and many others. Decolonization was not "truly the creation of the new man," and it quite obviously did not create a "cultural clean slate" (Fanon 1963, 2). It is worth considering that more people were butchered after liberating and empowering revolutions than during colonial rule.

Freire shared Fanon's goals and mood, although somewhat softened, but he provided a better yet still undetailed sense of a solution. His four dialogical processes of liberationist organizing (the revolutionary or empowerment process) attack the tactics of oppression—conquest, divide and rule, manipulation, and cultural invasion—with the virtues of cooperation, unity, organization, and cultural synthesis. Fidel Castro is his primary example of the successful dialogical hero, although Freire's enthusiasm for the Castro regime ignored its oppressive tendencies, which were evident even during its first decade (Laqueur 2002; Horowitz and Suchlicki 2003).

Like Fanon, Freire (1970) underestimated and indeed ignored the problems of postcolonial state tyranny. His pardon for postrevolutionary brutality—"the act of rebellion by the oppressed (an act which is always or nearly always as violent as the initial violence of the oppressors) can initiate love"—may have also excused scrutiny of revolutions in the people's name (Freire 1970, 38).

Freire (1970) designed adult literacy education as "the practice of freedom," a core tactic in the central strategy to empower the poor in Brazil. It was initially tested in the Adult Education Project of the

Movement of Popular culture in Recife, Brazil, during the 1950s and early 1960s. Freire was the program's coordinator. Literacy was the central tactic in the strategy of creating a revolutionary constituency among the oppressed in Brazil.

> From the beginning, we rejected the hypothesis of a purely mechanistic literacy program and considered the problem of teaching adults how to read in relation to the awakening of their consciousness. We wished to design a project in which we would attempt to move from naïveté to a critical attitude at the same time we taught reading. (Freire 1970, 43)

The critical attitude to be taught through the process of "conscientization" was grounded in individualism and democracy and clearly intended to revolutionize the political and social system. Conscientization implied a dialogue of deep respect and equality with a teacher whose preparations made the educational process germane to the immediate situation of the person to acquire literacy. The student was empowered first by assuming responsibility for his or her own literacy and then by the power of communication that literacy conferred. The right thinking of the acquired critical attitude—consciousness-raising—would naturally lead to deep social change through the radicalization of the multitude of the poor and oppressed.

> Radicalization involves increased commitment to the position one has chosen. It is predominantly critical, loving, humble, and communicative, and therefore a positive stance. (Freire 1970, 10)

Adult literacy and liberationist organizing, let alone an impassioned dedication to the welfare of oppressed peasants and the poor, is apparently not enough. Freire's efforts failed and his liberationist organizing plan mirrors the standard, amorphous social problem-solving processes and clichés of community organization. Conscientization and revolutionary organizing have rarely, if ever, overcome peasant resistance to forming a viable political opposition, and they did not in Brazil. Indeed, Freire's astute enumeration of implacable, if not actually, reactionary peasant attitudes—fatalism and self-depreciation but notably "the irresistible attraction towards the oppressors and their way of life" (Freire 1973, 44)—goes far to explain their own subjugation. Indeed, the fact that peasants voluntarily consent to and take pleasure in their cultures expresses their "overpowering aspiration" to maintain it and to resist empowerment (ibid., 44). The Pedagogy of the Oppressed offers no specific steps to overcome those attitudes nor does Freire cite routine success in empowering peasants and the poor.

Freire's literacy program was terminated by the 1964 military coup in Brazil that also resulted in his exile. Revolution was cancelled by bureaucratic decree, highlighting the deficiencies of empowerment radicalism. His program to radicalize the poor and oppressed, conducted under public auspices, apparently assumed that it would be continued by those to be overthrown. He never made provisions for handling the basic steps of forming a revolutionary cadre that was independent of the very authorities who were to be eliminated by the revolution or, more broadly, to develop support for transforming a society from within that society itself. Humble love exerts little power.

Democracy and literacy do not by themselves imply any content aside from enacting the will of the people and an ability to read and communicate. The essential values of a society and the content of communication are not prescriptions of democracy and literacy. Freire does not describe the outcomes of the program: the number taught to read and write, the number radicalized, and so forth. But, at a minimum, its insurgent message was clear to the Brazilian generals who took charge. Moreover, Freire's education for critical consciousness was not nearly as open-ended, participatory, and respectfully humble as it pretends to be. It was a tactic of radicalization and not by itself a goal of learning. It came to transmit its own sense of society, justice, and change. Shorn of its ethereal goodness, it seems about as manipulative as common political intervention but more sanctimonious and perhaps less successful. If the impulse to revolution or reform includes greater material equality, then its practice requires more than the razzle-dazzle of empowerment consciousness raising.

Despite its consistent failures, the radical tradition inspired empowerment practice among the helping professions, caring constituency, and empaths of the United States in a variety of ways. It converted the marginal and poor into the oppressed and the colonized, excused violence or at least grievance procedures outside of the established system as tactics of reform, and more subtly allowed the poignancy of need to compensate for the lack of a program of empowerment.

A grave problem of hypocrisy arises when the practice of empowerment becomes the antithesis of its inspirational mass movements, undercutting liberation and the pursuit of equality with the conciliatory processes of adaptation. This is the condition of contemporary empowerment practice. It has retreated from politics and social development, becoming complicit as symbol and ceremony with the very society it pretends to transform.

The Practice of Black Empowerment

Barbara Solomon's (1976) early and influential *Black Empowerment*, among the initial attempts to define a dedicated practice of empowerment for blacks, mirrored the mood of Friere and Fanon, although without Fanon's appetite for violent insurrection. Yet, whatever its roots in mass movements and social need, modern empowerment practice must stand on its own as a defensible professional intervention. This implies credible evidence of routine effectiveness. Accepting this obligation, *Black Empowerment* claims to present "more effective strategies for helping clients in black communities achieve personal and collective goals (1)." *Black Empowerment* inspired similar programs for Hispanics, women, gays, and other supposedly oppressed groups. Each approach apparently justifies its uniqueness, its dedicated approach to particular groups on grounds of their subcultural differences, beliefs, values, and embedded habits, which distinguish one group from the others and thereby necessitate unique worker skills or interventions and segregated practices.

Solomon argues that successful empowerment practice in black communities entails nonracist practitioners who engage the black "client system" by "capturing their imagination," "establishing rapport," "establishing expertise," "assessing client strengths," "establishing the client as agent of change," and throughout handling resistance to change. Similar to Freire, Solomon's empowerment process employs the common elements of planned problem solving adopted by community organization and communication theory, among others: engaging the community in a process of identifying goals and then working toward their achievement by involving local leadership. More to the point, there is nothing in Solomon's empowerment practice that requires a distinct approach to blacks, while the basic reliance on community practice lacks substantial testimony to an ability to achieve its goals.

Ignoring for the moment the questionable effectiveness of empowerment practice and community practice generally, Solomon fails to identify the special conditions of the black community that justify a dedicated approach. Indeed, it is baffling that Solomon acknowledges, apart from skin color and a legacy of prejudice, the inability to distinguish poor black communities from any other poor and needy group but still pushes on to argue for a special approach to their empowerment. In itself, black inequality does not justify a special approach to blacks. Thus, Solomon raises the question "whether or not blacks in the United States are *culturally* distinctive from other racial or ethnic groups" (48) but then, succeeds in rejecting each attempt to do so (48–53). She does the same in considering whether the black community has "defining characteristics," citing Levine and Campbell's (1972) five variables that "no longer deny validity to the concept of black community," notably a shared ethnic ideology (quoted in Solomon, 66).

Solomon asserts that "there is considerable evidence that black communities exist at least in an ideological and even geographical sense" (67). While it is obvious that blacks are not randomly interspersed throughout America, geographic concentration by itself does not constitute community. Shared ideology may constitute community, especially a subgroup ideology that differs from dominant ideology. Solomon never defines the content of black ideology but rather only the conditions of black inequality. She assumes that prejudice against blacks is sufficient to define them as a community. Still, it is not clear whether racism unites people in a community or simply defines them demographically as the victims of prejudice. Solomon does not show how a shared sense of injustice constitutes a shared ideology that then justifies a separate approach to empowerment.

Graham (2002) observes that "historically, social welfare activities in black communities have been tethered to social, religious, and political organizations and have been a major source of support for individuals and families in the struggle for survival and resistance amidst times of hardship and deep seated racism . . ." (37). True but the same can be said of almost any community that has suffered systematic prejudicial discrimination within a larger society. Even the more compelling idea that the identity of an oppressed people emerges from a collective struggle is generally a characteristic of all groups in conflict (Coser 1956). Thus, the likelihood that "affiliations across political, social and religious groups [that] serve an important empowerment function in the black community" does not translate into an empowerment practice devoted to blacks (Graham 2002, 38). Rather, it suggests only a tactical consideration of whether separate empowerment strategies are more effective than inclusive strategies.

Similarly, Denby, Rocha, and Kane (2004) fail to derive successful "best practices" from their review of "the research literature on mental health services to African Americans" (73), a body of information as weak as the general material concerning psychotherapy and mental health care (discussed later in the chapter). Best practice remains indeterminate practice, at best.[1] The evasion of credible methods says much about the role and motives of empowerment practice in the United States. Contrary to their argument, "culturally defined programming" is not "evident due to the prevalence and complexity of African Americans' health needs" (ibid.). Arguments based on invented and imagined special characteristics of blacks justify a pernicious process of resegregating them, this time through social services and the arguments of black professionals. Even Denby, Rocha, and Kane's (2004) structural argument that the mental problems of blacks emerge from prejudicial discrimination (e.g., poverty and cultural bias), which creates stress, is consistent with other groups of poor and marginalized Americans. Yet, the authors go on to recommend "a cooperative living program model for African American families"—not all families with similar problems but only African-American families. The logic of a therapeutic approach to segregation presumably permits Catholics, Jews, Moslems, Hispanics, French, and so on to also appropriate public funds for separate treatments and clinics and hospitals for services reserved to specific religions, ethnicities, races, or genders. As an extension, it would seem also justifiable for black parents to deny their children the opportunity to form friendships with white children so as to strengthen their black identity, thus reestablishing the viability of segregated schools and eventually segregated housing, employment, and the like. The barriers to transforming a diverse nation into a productive culture are substantial, not least because the intended beneficiaries—the victims of prejudicial discrimination—have often been more influenced by Stockholm syndrome than by notions of decency.

It is worth recalling Wilson's (1978) prescient observation that socioeconomic class has eclipsed race as a salient factor in explaining stratification in the United States. To the extent to which Wilson is accurate—which is given substantial support by the fact of a black president of the United States—the declining significance of race marks the tradition of social work and the helping professions staying about two generations behind social need and prevailing progressive ideology. Indeed, this lag in relevance testifies to the compatibility of empowerment practice with conservative politics.[2]

Since the elimination of de jure discrimination in the United States, blacks have gradually lost standing as unique victims of injustice and economic inequality; the inequities of class encompass a much greater segment of the population than blacks. Blacks present a heterogeneous experience that supervenes race as a point of communal and personal identity—employment status, occupation, gender, region, health, and so forth—rather than one that is encompassed within a communal ideology of discrimination. Indeed, blacks seem to be following the experience of most ethnic and racial subgroups in the Unites States, adapting to the prevailing culture on its terms and proceeding to differentiate itself along classic lines of social status, income, education, and the like. Moreover, the moral judgments it imposes on itself—the worthy and the unworthy, the motivated and the lazy, the virtuous and the sinful, the provident and the impulsive, the winners and the losers, the upwardly mobile and the persistently miscreant—seem the bedrock of the American ethos rather than some distinct subgroup ideology.[3] In this regard, Wilson's comments about the declining influence of race also pertain to the black community itself. The perpetuation of race-based interventions such as Affirmative Action policies and the continuing politics of race (distinguished from need-based interventions and the politics of class) raise questions beyond the pragmatic issue of effectiveness about symbolism displacing material reform.

The socioeconomic misfortunes and the political disadvantages of the black community are shared by other groups, notably poor whites. Moreover, Solomon does not argue that the historical subjugation of American blacks, first as slaves and then through American apartheid, has created unique challenges for empowerment practice. As with the previous radical tradition, black empowerment seems more ideological—an attempt to justify attention to the needs of a particular group—than programmatic. However, black empowerment, by invoking a specialness of ineffable characteristics, raises barriers that isolate needy groups from each other. More to the point, indefinable group characteristics that justify special treatment constitute the essence of bigotry, the spectral proofs of contemporary American sin and virtue.

Solomon provides little systematic support for black empowerment practice. She typically sustains its value with other ideological works that address the virtue of the goal more than the means to realize it.

Her tatters of evidence include a few case studies, some memoirist reportage, and even an unpublished master's thesis. Indeed, attempts to test black empowerment practice are sparse, weak, and, in the end, distorted to underwrite an improbable and ineffective reliance on self-help within the black community.

Leashore, McMurray, and Bailey's (1991) experiment in family re-unification and preservation, Volunteers for Children in Need (VCIN), exemplifies the problem. VCIN assumed that "inadequate resources and supportive services continue to be barriers to family reunifica-tion and preservation, especially for families of color" (252) and that those resources could be provided through "a community-based volunteer network to help reunite African American children in the foster care system [of Washington, DC] with their natural families" (252): Among other activities, VCIN went about recruiting voluntary, community-based groups, strengthening the ability of these organiza-tions to develop resources, and establishing links between the project's volunteers and child welfare agencies. Drawing from Solomon (1976) among others, "the project's conceptual framework of empowerment emphasized a family-centered approach for problem resolution and family stabilization" (255).

Potential families were carefully screened for those who "expressed strong desires to be reunited with their children" ... [and] "strong bonds between children and their families existed despite placement in foster care" (257). In the end, the sixty-two black families and their 115 children in foster care who were enrolled in VCIN were probably the most likely to be reunited among the many thousands of families and children in the Washington, DC, foster care system at the time. VCIN provided priority access to housing, medical care, donations of furniture, clothing, and food; ancillary services such as counseling and recreation; some job referral assistance; and other services (although the amount of services actually received by the families and children is not reported). Moreover, most of the families were also receiving public assistance.

In the end, VCIN succeeded in reuniting only eighteen of its sixty-two target families. Nonetheless, the authors concluded that

> the family reunification project at the Howard University School of Social Work demonstrated that African American children placed in foster care can be reunited with their families without jeopardizing their welfare. The project also demonstrated that African American

> voluntary groups, organizations, and individuals can help these families by providing tangible and intangible resources. (Leashore, McMurray, and Bailey's 1991, 262).

In fact, the experiment demonstrated just the reverse, that the resources of a poor community and its voluntary contributions are inadequate to handle the serious material deficits of its members. The good wishes of communal self-help are inadequate even for those families with the greatest motivation and the fewest barriers to reunification. The project contained no control group, and it seems likely that in the customary course of events a similar number of these families would have been reunited. VCIN empowered hardly anyone at all except those who fashion careers out of activities that subvert attention to deprivation by promoting self-help among the poor. Moreover, empowerment programs that fail to empower deprive the poor of sophisticated advocacy and in the case of VCIN, deny the devastation of American apartheid and poverty. Self-help may be consistent with the nation's romantic sense of heroic individualism, but it quite apparently failed in VCIN to help poor black people set up a home for themselves and their children. It is revealing that the authors, housed in the nation's most prominent historically black university, came to tout self-help in place of raising a ruckus about American inequalities.

A program in New York City developed a curriculum to empower African American grandparents who cared for their grandchildren (Cox 2002). Fifteen of the most motivated and capable grandparents were recruited to participate in the program from among forty members of a support group in a counseling agency; fourteen completed the course. The goals—"to strengthen the parenting skills of the grandparents and to increase their effectiveness in the community as advocates for themselves and for other grandparents raising grandchildren" (Cox 2002, 47)—were pursued through twelve three-hour classes over six weeks held at a prominent school of social work. The classes covered a variety of topics related to child rearing and empowerment. The students were given homework to apply the lessons to their own lives and report on their experiences during subsequent sessions.

The grandparents were apparently very satisfied with the program and according to Cox, carried the skills they learned into their community along with the message of empowerment. There was no objective evaluation, comparison group, or long-term and direct evaluation of the grandparents' improved skills with their grandchildren. In spite of the selective sample and the absence of credible evaluative methods, Cox concludes that "grandparents are eager to learn and willing to participate in programs that can enhance their skills and ease their situation" (53). This is how missionaries brag to their congregations.

Similarly, without any objective evaluation or quantitative analysis, Manning, Cornelius, and Okundaye (2004) insist that their empowerment program provides "a culturally competent, practical social work approach that facilitates the well-being of African Americans" (229). This requires the social worker to

> support the development of a strong cultural and racial identification by enhancing ego development. The social worker who uses ego psychology as a theoretical framework can easily incorporate empowerment, Afrocentric, and spiritual concepts. Through the therapeutic process, the client internalizes a more stable identification with his or her culture and race while developing new coping strategies for dealing with oppressive environments. (Manning, Cornelius and Okundaye 2004, 234)

The authors do not support the effectiveness of their approach with reference to credible research nor do they evaluate the quality of the research they rely on. Nonetheless, they conclude without any empirical test that the integration of an Afrocentric perspective, ego psychology, and spirituality is therapeutic. Indeed, they suggest that a stronger ethnic and racial identity is important for the mental health of blacks. They also seem to be promulgating a stereotype of blacks that largely ignores their pragmatic, rational capacity while imposing on the black community a racial rigidity perhaps unneeded and unwise. Again, the tacit political assumption that black identity is more important than the role of the citizen may isolate the black community from similarly needy groups. An Afrocentric empowerment practice insists on black identity when the crushing need for it has given way to an open society whose injustices are related more to inequality than to political and social oppression.

Chadiha et al. (2004) also sidestep direct empirical tests, again relying on their reading of the literature to recommend three practice strategies to empower African-American women who are informal caregivers. However, their discussion of the needs of these women fails in any way to distinguish their characteristics from female caregivers who are not African American. The insistence on ethnicity and race probably expresses the authors' preferences more than an objective condition that justifies separate attention to the deprivations of different groups.

Among the most sophisticated empowerment practice outcome studies—employing a randomized design, double blinding, and quantitative analysis—Kaslow et al. (2010) studied the effects of two forms of psychological interventions on suicidal and abused African-American women. The experimental intervention was a "culturally informed, empowerment-focused psychological group intervention" (450). The authors reported varied but weak outcomes, acknowledging that "the intervention was not as successful as anticipated" (455). Even these modest results were impaired by a number of methodological problems—large attrition, the absence of diagnostic interviews, self-reports from the women without objective checks, and the absence of direct observations of behaviors such as coping skills.

More to the point, the intervention did not address the crucial empowerment issue: whether the women were empowered to terminate their abusive situations. Psychological interventions typically substitute the improbable goal of self-help not only for situations that, as the authors state, require "large-scale community-wide prevention programs" but also for programs that can address the needs of victims for safety. If anything, Kaslow et al. (2010) demonstrated the futility of addressing serious abuse with bootstrapping, education, and self-realization.

The experimental intervention

> builds on the strengths of African American women, their families and communities (e.g. achievement oriented, strong work orientation, strong kinship bonds, flexible family roles, strong religious orientation). The group format has been advocated for African American women; it provides the opportunity to build networks for emotional and spiritual support, promote positive health, and share stories and obtain validation. (Kaslow et al. 2010, 452)

Yet, these would appear to be the general characteristics of a multitude of different ethnic, racial, and gender groups in the United States, even white Anglo-Saxon Protestant men, and other successful ethnicities. The rationale for employing groups in treatment is not culturally unique but similar for most other people. However, "achievement orientation" and the others are decidedly not the strengths of the treatment population whose lives the authors characterized as "chaotic and traumatic . . . unstable," and fraught with many psychological difficulties. It appears that the intervention was designed for a stereotype of black women but applied to very different, far needier, black women. Their principal similarity was being black.

The program's culturally sensitive content included

> African proverbs, attends to African American heroines and per-
> sonal positive female mentors and role models, and emphasizes
> culturally relevant coping strategies (spirituality, religious involve-
> ment) to enhance self awareness and connection. For example, in
> the meeting devoted to enhancing intrapersonal protective factors,
> the women are asked to draw images that depict themselves as an
> African American goddess, as well as to collectively call out names
> of African American heroines and personal female positive mentors
> and role models to assist them in experiencing themselves as strong
> African American women. (Kaslow et al. 2010, 451)

The intervention appears more concerned with African-American identity than with successful treatment, especially as little, if any, evidence exists to sustain the effectiveness of race-based psychotherapy let alone race-based empowerment treatment. The authors created a fantasy of personal identity for women with little, if any, ethnic ties to African culture while assuming that the pageantry of black female martyrs to American apartheid, cultural icons, and personal role models are any more germane than ties to the broader American culture. Indeed, this sort of Afrocentric nationalism also reduces the possibility of successful outcomes by separating abused and suicidal African-American women from the much larger constituency afflicted with the same problems. The research makes the normative statement that abused black women should feel a stronger bond with the authors' notion of the American blacks without ever inquiring into actual preferences of abused black women themselves.

Kaslow et al. (2010) deal with drama rather than with credible science and successful psychotherapy. As fiction, the drama plays into the unfortunate imagery of blacks as fundamentally unique and often deviant from the American tradition when, in fact, their needs and their strengths—even as depicted by the authors—seem to coincide with the common cultural choices of the nation.

Following Kaslow et al.'s (2010) logic of ethnocentric therapy for victims of interpersonal violence, abused fourth-generation Italian Americans would listen to Verdi operas, look at Michelangelo paintings, and emulate Lady Gaga, Rudolph Guliani, Francis Ford Coppola, Lee Iacocca, and Joe Torre. As part of their empowerment treatment, assimilated Jews would be required to wear skull caps and frock coats, learn Yiddish, and take courses in nuclear physics. Chinese Americans would practice foot binding and kowtowing. This would continue as the victims of violence are entertained in pursuit of empowerment by the pleasures of bigotry until spear-chucker empowerment practice reduces the powerless to museum-quality aboriginals. Sometimes, the cure is worse than the disease.

Black empowerment practice pursues two historical traditions. On the one hand, it aspires to engage with the dominant white society to improve the conditions of blacks—the tradition of Dubois, Mandela, and Martin Luther King to name a few. On the other hand, it seeks to strengthen subcultural separateness in the tradition exemplified by the Nation of Islam, Marcus Garvey, and perhaps even Booker T. Washington. The tradition of separation assumes that the dominant white society is implacably racist, and, thus, rejects assimilation, retreating into subcultural protections, self-reliance, and self-help. Yet, contemporary black empowerment practice fails at both social reform and self-improvement; it neither teaches program recipients to compete successfully for money, status, and power nor transfers self-help skills to them. The impressive political and social gains of the black community since World War II occurred through mass movements and political struggles within American society that were not influenced by black empowerment practice or its programs. However, black empowerment practice shies away from political conflict on behalf of greater equality preferring self-help approaches that are consistent with American social welfare policy to remedy personal deficiencies.

The failure of black communal self-sufficiency occurs within the broader failure of a professional community practice of any sort—community development, community organization, neighborhood planning and problem solving, community psychology, and other forms of small-scale self-help for poor and needy communities—that attempts to address substantial local problems with local resources. In fact, the absence of local resources, including political strength, leadership, and skill to affect conditions that are largely the result of broader influences, erects an insurmountable barrier to community practice in impoverished communities. In spite of the proliferation of black empowerment practice, economic inequality of poor blacks and perhaps even their geographic and social isolation have increased steadily in the United States since the early 1970s (Mazumber 2005; Jantti 2006; Burtless 2007). Empowerment practice that insists on the centrality of self-help among American blacks denies centuries of prejudicial discrimination as well as the problems of class in America.

Empowering Women of Color

Gutierrez (1990) extended Solomon's (1976) factional approach from black empowerment to women of color generally: black, Hispanic, Asian, and Native American. She also carried along the same problems that beset black empowerment. Gutierrez defines empowerment practice as benefiting from a synergism between the individual and the group to affect individual, interpersonal, and institutional change; empowerment includes a sense of personal control, the ability to affect others' behavior, community change, the better distribution of resources, and other goals (Gutierrez 1990, 150). She then goes on to identify four psychological changes that are "crucial" to move the individual to action. The empowerment process itself includes critical techniques: accepting the individual's definition of the problem, building upon his or her strengths, a "power analysis" of the individual's problems, teaching specific skills, developing resources and advocating for the individual (151).

Gutierrez presses her central assumption that "social problems stem not from individual deficits, but rather from the failure of the society to meet the needs of all its members" (150). She then goes on to justify empowerment practice by the "powerlessness and oppression of women of color" (152). However, her process of empowerment appears to begin with individual change that presumes the ability of beleaguered women to heroically overcome their oppressive environments. Aside from the paradox of the overwhelmed not actually being overwhelmed, Gutierrez's empowerment process is quintessentially romantic, inventing capacities where there are none and more to the point relying on a process that is essentially self-help, although with some professional assistance. In this way, empowerment practice became little more than consciousness raising, reeducation, and psychotherapy—three forms that have been customarily ineffective and occasionally barbaric. Moreover, the promotion of an ineffective form that impedes the search for more effective solutions raises questions about professional motives and responsibility.

Gutierrez engages in the fiction of self-determination by insisting that the empowerment worker accept the individual's definition of the problem. However, her article pays tribute to the fact that empowerment practice begins with the assumptions of powerlessness,

oppression, and structural causation and proceeds through interme-
diary steps to disabuse the individual of an errant sense of her own
problems. This is disingenuous but characteristic of empowerment
theory that with blithe dexterity holds incompatible tenets of practice:
on the one hand, the grievous conditions of political, social, economic,
and psychological deprivation that lead to the serious incapacities of
the powerless; but on the other hand, their pliancy and inherent wisdom, and the overarching ability of vague problem-solving processes
to succeed. Moreover, the factional assumption of empowerment
practice—that women of color constitute a compelling community
of need—substitutes ethnicity and gender for class and the theorist's
sense of the world for that of her powerless patients. While defining
the material deficits of women of color, Gutierrez assumes that their
gender identity is more germane than their class identity as poor. Indeed, it is more likely that many, if not most, poor women primarily
identify themselves within a community that also includes men and
children to whom they are related by blood, proximity, and affection
rather than simply as victims of abuse, patriarchy, and their own misguided loyalties.

The criticisms might lose most of their force if Gutierrez (1990)
produced credible evidence that her factional approach to need
was more than ideological foot-stomping. However, empowerment
practice for women of color apparently does not resolve their many
problems. Gutierrez (1990) cannot cite strong evidence to sustain her
empowerment process, and the subsequent literature provides no
greater support for the notion that poor and marginal women of color
can be effectively empowered to handle their own personal problems,
let alone to repair the structural deficits of society.

Among Gutierrez's cited support, Rappaport (1981) writes that
empowerment ideology "demands that we find ways to take what we
learn from . . . diverse settings and solutions and make it more public,
so as to help foster social policies and programs that make it more
rather than less likely that others not now handling their own problems in living or shut out from current solutions, gain control over
their lives" (ibid., 15). In a manner that is typical of the empowerment
literature, Rappaport goes on to discuss a variety of sources that agree
that empowerment is a worthwhile goal, but he fails to put forward
evidence that empowerment practice has been successful. At best, he
simply cites sources asserting that feelings such as efficacy matter "a
great deal to people"; but, none of Rappaport's sources demonstrate

that feelings of efficacy can be induced through empowerment practice nor, more importantly, that they precede behaviors of empowerment (ibid., 18). Furthermore, Rappaport's data do not appear to be immediately relevant to the intended beneficiaries of empowerment practice.

Similarly, Pinderhughes (1983) argues that empowerment "treatment should focus not only on strengthening ego functioning and family structure but also upon reinforcing the appropriate support of group, community and other social systems" (334). Pinderhughes' suggestions are not paired with evidence that sustains them but once again, she simply cites compatible opinions. In addition, "strengthening ego function" is largely devoid of a systematic ability to predict successful outcomes from psychotherapy. In contrast, real achievement, perhaps the result of extraordinarily expensive structural investments, may be a more effective strategy to improve self-esteem, although one that has rarely been considered in the United States for poorer citizens.

Gutierrez's argument relies on a faulty base of research. In the rare cases where it offers empirical evidence, its methods undercut its conclusions (Janoff-Bulman 1979). The largest portion of Gutierrez's cited support constitutes a weak convergent literature of agreement that offers little, if any, empirical support for empowerment practice itself aside from poorly researched case studies and journalistic anecdotes (Resnick 1976; Pearlin and Schooler 1978; Keefe 1980; Longres and McLeod 1980; Sherman and Winocur 1983; Simmons and Parsons 1983; Shapiro 1984; Garvin 1985; Hirayama and Hirayama 1985; Pernell 1985; Gould 1987; Hasenfeld 1987; Morell 1987; Kopacsi and Faulkner 1988). Gutierrez simply ignores Thoits' (1983) rare voice of skepticism except to cite the piece in support of the conclusion that "powerlessness is the source of higher mental illness among the poor, women, and members of ethnic and racial minority groups" (Gutierrez, 149). Yet, Thoits' (1983) extensive critique of the relevant literature, pointing to its debilitating methodological pitfalls, leads at most to tentative speculations about the causes of powerlessness rather than to justification for empowerment practice itself. The only conclusion that seems warranted, even while it does not spring logically from Thoits' analysis, is both trivial and a truism of any human behavior: "despite its methodological limitations ... life events research has still taught us something at once simple and profound: the etiology of mental illness is partially environmental or social in origin" (Thoits, 87). Indeed, it would be difficult to identify anyone who denied at least

33

a partial social influence over mental illness. With little surprise, this insight has not led to effective treatments.

Gutierrez also ignores a number of substantial challenges to the success of her empowerment strategies that arise within her base of research. Kopacsi and Faulkner (1988) point to the elitism of the women's movement and its irrelevance to the political and social aspirations of beleaguered women. In fact, the empowerment of less needy women seems to have taken the heart out of the empowerment of the very needy. Pearlin and Schooler (1978) suggest that coping strength—the capacity for empowerment—is greatest when dealing with immediate personal areas and least effective not only in "impersonal" areas such as employment but also, by extension, in political and social spheres.

By itself, the absence of evidence for effective empowerment practice in Gutierrez's references should have drawn considerable commentary. Instead, Gutierrez's strong conclusions are tributes to ideological commitment and ideological symbolism, but they do not sustain empowerment practice for women of color. If anything, the empty literature suggests that the weak approaches of modern empowerment practice are incapable of dispelling feelings of futility and engendering behaviors that improve people's lot. The weakness of the empowerment practice literature subsequent to Gutierrez (1990) sustains the same conclusion and reprises skepticism toward any planned professional intervention to empower beleaguered people.

While Gutierrez (1990) continues to be frequently cited in both textbooks and research on empowerment practice, there are hardly any subsequent evaluations of practice with women of color per se. The absence suggests that "women of color" do not comprise a viable group for liberation through empowerment practice. Apparently, oppressed women who are black, Asian, Hispanic, and Native American do not find a common cause and are unwilling to participate with each other. In fact, the literature reports a few interventions with mixed groups of women. Empowerment practice for women of color apparently prefers to separate women of color into ethnically and racially homogeneous groups.[4]

Empowering women of color and empowerment generally are initially practices of attitude change through some form of talk therapy to raise consciousness of oppression and powerlessness. Chaiklin (2011) challenges the plausibility of this approach with evidence that attitude change is not a precondition of behavioral change. Indeed, Chaiklin's conclusions challenge all of the empowerment strategies that attempt to employ tactics of conscientization, that is, the multitude of interventions of political and personal consciousness raising (Resnick 1976). More to the point, the empowerment theorists have uniformly failed to demonstrate the systematic efficacy of consciousness raising or attitude change.

The long persistence of powerlessness among needy people belies the assurances of the cozened and secure revolutionary that a new consciousness is an irresistible force of justice. If the weak in the United States were truly incapacitated by oppressive conditions, then perhaps a cadre of farsighted revolutionaries might stimulate their revolt with heroic deeds of their own in emulation of Mao, Lenin, Castro, El Cid, Simon Bolivar, or Joan of Arc. Instead of personal risk, Gutierrez (1990) shelters in professionalism, invoking the techniques of psychotherapy, community organization, community planning, and the like but ignoring their routine insufficiencies.

Empowering Women

Much of the success of the women's movement has been romanticized as heroic overcoming—acts of irresistible will and intelligence—that is blind to the context of large gains in American gender equality (Cohen 1988; Shreve 1989; Berkeley 1999; Rodnitzky 1999; Maxwell 2009; Giardina 2010). "The fires lit by the movement blazed so intensely that even the powerful backlash of conservatism and religious fundamentalism that gained power in the United States since the 1970s could not extinguish the impact of Women's Liberation or dull the desire for freedom in the hearts and minds of women" (Giardina 2010, 243).[5]

Yet, rather than a mass movement led by cadres of dedicated revolutionaries and expressed through the practice of feminist empowerment, greater gender equality in the United States emerged as the society has slowly grown toward universal enfranchisement, hyperdemocracy, procedural equality, and a national culture that transcended regional and subcultural differences. The redefinition of gender roles realizes changing economic and social realities, notably two-earner families and increasingly undifferentiated parenting roles. Heroic self-invention and transformative leadership are the theatrics of the change but probably not its cause. Change did not take place through the deep self-realizations of introspective epiphanies but rather because highly differentiated gender roles in society and the family lost their purpose. Ideology, that is social preferences, accommodated socioeconomic reality and only weakly shaped that reality. In other words, new behaviors preceded changed attitudes, and social tolerances adapted to the changed reality (Chaiklin 2011).

While associated with changing gender roles, the women's movement has still conserved basic American social institutions, largely replicating American stratification without challenging the fairness and decency of American institutions except as they deny equal access to women. It is telling that as the feminist agenda for equality was increasingly realized, membership in feminist organizations declined. In explaining the decline, Maxwell (2009) argues that the current feminist

> movement does not appeal to women, even though they are happy it existed at one point in time. Women generally feel they benefited from the feminists of the Friedan era, but no longer see a need for the movement to continue. (Maxwell 2009, 105)

Perhaps too the decline in membership and enthusiasm for the feminist agenda among women may be "a welcome reconsideration of whether women's interests are best served by deploying an ideology which affirms gender differences and presents them as natural and immutable" (Echols 1989, 294).

Women's demand for equal participation—the mantra of equal pay for equal work—largely pursues a procedural reform rather than substantive reallocation of resources through public policy. Feminist practice to empower women compromises with greater material concern for poorer women. Similar to empowerment practice generally, feminist empowerment practice is reduced to ceremonies of equality with a focus on self-actualization through psychotherapeutic exchanges and to rituals of material provision. Adaptation to the new equality of women—the ability to take on the power roles traditionally allotted to men, notably in the marketplace and politics—has superseded the problems of socioeconomic insufficiency. In this way, the American women most in need of liberation from the strictures of deprivation, perhaps more than half of all women, have largely been ignored by the feminist movement. Equal empowerment with men is less of a need for most women than greater empowerment measured by their family incomes and access to social services. In particular, day care, child education, vocational training, income support, health and mental health care, and even respite care of one sort or another open opportunities for more women than improving the socioeconomic mobility of the relatively few well educated and well placed. It is no accident that the leading organization of women, the National Organization of Women, gives priority to the mobility of the already advantaged and that the nine-to-five type of organizations—labor unions of largely lower-paid and vulnerable women—have foundered.

The rich literature of gender equality often comments on the unfortunate elitism of the women's movement in the United States, its concentration on merit rather than redistribution (Kopacsi and Faulken 1988; Brenner 2000; Maxwell 2009). However, the intellectual life of the movement is reluctant to consider that its elitism is sanctioned broadly as a true expression of women's priorities, or that the movement's elitism is itself false consciousness. Indeed, oppression may be more ascribed to beleaguered women than accepted by them. Nonfeminist American women may be deluded both in their role choices as well as in their social values, but their choices have been uncoerced. Quite pointedly, empowerment practice has not demonstrated any influence on these choices.

Empowerment practice to liberate women from the oppression of material deprivation and the remnants of patriarchy has given way to the narcissism of psychological liberation. That empowerment practice for women has failed at all three suggests its persistence more as symbol and street theater than as pragmatic social service. Indeed, the faint effort to evaluate the outcomes either of services for true female victims—as examples, shelters and treatment for battered women—or for the customary empowerment practice for women suggests that the social meaning of empowerment practice for women, similar to a cross on a church, lies more in its expressive presence than in its material effects. The small attention to outcomes also suggests that empowerment practice has always been marginal to the political activism of the feminist movement and perhaps even peripheral to its sense of women's needs.

"The De Madres a Madres program was initiated to decrease barriers and increase access to prenatal care" (McFarlane and Fehir 1994, 389). It participated with a variety of health providers to reach out to pregnant women in one of Houston's Hispanic neighborhoods. On the basis of "interviews, which are informal and consist of simply conversing with anyone associated with the program," De Madres a Madres was apparently successful (390). Access increased, the number of low-birth-weight babies declined, and health information was widely distributed. Yet, the program claims empowerment beyond simply a successful outreach program: "outcome data identified the covert functions of the program to be the enhancement of individual women's self-esteem, power, and economy ... the theoretical basis for empowerment of women" (381). The data for the conclusion of empowerment are anecdotal, coming from interviews with five volunteer women who in the absence of De Madres a Madres may well have sought out on their own similar volunteer experiences to gain the same benefits of self-esteem and personal power, while the transfer of the gains to "the economy" of the community remains speculative and undocumented. Moreover, the evaluation lacks any controls, and, thus, it is not clear what value De Madres a Madres provided in addition to the efforts of the health providers themselves to reach out to the community. Still and all, the issue is empowerment, but the program's evaluation methods cannot respond credibly.

Parsons (2001) reports on empowerment practice with a total of fifteen women in two groups intended to reduce their oppression by increasing their voice and decreasing their isolation and alienation. Parsons attended sessions, interviewed participants, and claimed that the strategies were impressively effective. That was it—no measurement, no inter-rater reliability checks, just Parsons and her notes.

Two studies discuss empowerment with substance-abusing women. Lafave, Desportes, and McBride (2009) tested the perceptions of empowerment of fifty women who were current or former patients in a substance-abuse day treatment program. The women reported major gains in measures of empowerment, that is, taking more responsibility for themselves in life skills, finance, leisure, relationships, and others. However, the authors neither bother to evaluate the accuracy of the claims nor do they include controls of similar women who did not go through day treatment. Most curious, there is neither any mention of whether the women ceased abusing alcohol and drugs nor is there any awareness that patient biases may account for their hopeful reports rather than any change in actual behavior.

Gollub et al. (2010) employed a randomized design—rare in the evaluation of empowerment practice—in testing an educational approach to prevent HIV infection among drug-abusing women. They concluded that four sessions of an interactive educational approach stressing body knowledge and HIV prevention were superior to HIV counseling and testing. All the outcome measures depended on responses to questions testing knowledge or self-reports of behavior such as condom use. No measures were taken of HIV exposure itself—follow-up blood tests over years—nor did the authors bother to assess the reliability of responses. This is hardly substantial evidence to allow the authors to conclude that risks of HIV infection were reduced "based largely on women's solidarity and a focus on women's bodies as an independent route to empowerment, self-esteem, and reduction of risk behaviors among a marginalized population" (1711). Randomized designs are crucial, but they are never sufficient to assure the credibility of findings.[6]

Thus, it is understandable that the textbooks of feminist empowerment practice have little to refer to in handling outcomes. They hardly ever consider the effectiveness of their services, apparently content with the symbolic importance of feminist empowerment practice. *Building on Women's Strengths* (Peterson and Lieberman, editors, 2001) presents chapter after chapter assuming the effectiveness of "efforts to foster emancipatory change" (Weick in Peterson and Lieberman, 205) but presents no evidence that it has been achieved through empowerment practice. Each of the contributing authors simply cites those who agree with their position, but without evidence that the consensus has liberated anyone from sexism and patriarchy. The justice of their cause seems sufficient to justify empowerment practice.

The studied refusal to come to grips with the actual outcomes of practice is even more startling in *Feminist Practice in the 21st Century*, another textbook anthology devoted to social work's role in empowerment practice with women and published by the National Association of Social Workers (Van den Bergh 1995, which is little improved compared with Van den Bergh 1986). The chapter on feminist clinical social work by Land goes through the customary steps of listing sympathetic publications but fails to mention a single source that actually tests practice. "Feminist clinical practice is empowerment practice, although the means for psychotherapeutic growth may vary among feminist clinicians" (Land in Van den Bergh, 10). However, the absence of clinical evidence suggests that empowerment practice persists for reasons apart from its clinical prowess in achieving liberation. A clinical practice authorized by ideological conformity is a parody of the clinic and hints at cultishness. No chapter in Van den Bergh challenges this conclusion.[7]

The women's movement has realized many of its goals of gender equality but not because of empowerment practice and perhaps only incidentally as a result of its organized efforts. Empowerment practice has had little, if any, influence over social change in America. In fact, the heavy foot of psychotherapy that pervades feminist empowerment practice perversely reimagines the empowerment impulse to change society as a practice to change women. Psychotherapy locates the problem of resistance to change in women rather than in the sexist society. Of course, the literature argues that therapy is the vehicle of the revolutionary consciousness, the method by which to create cadres of change. However, hardly any of the feminist therapies set out clear goals beyond the desire for liberation, and none of them credibly demonstrated any achievements.

The success of the women's movement rests on the modesty of its goals—gender equality—and its acceptance of American stratification and perhaps even white privilege (Davis 1988).[8] Nevertheless, the accommodation with inequality belies any pretense to the empowerment of those women most in need of liberation.[9] Apparently, the feminist belief that sisterhood is sufficient for mobilizing empowerment may be counterproductive. The falloff of participation in feminist organizations may reflect both the sense that goals of equal access have been largely achieved and a sense that segregation by gender is a dead end. Unfortunately, the falloff may also signify a reluctance to address material deprivation and inequality. Certainly Faludi (1981) and Coontz (2011) among the majority of feminist authors suggest that the goals of feminism have not been achieved for many women. First-wave and second-wave feminism addressed material inequalities that still continue. Third-wave feminism is falling into the murk of postmodernist narcissism, the ineffable agenda of pleasure, psyche, and spirit. Feminist empowerment practice, perhaps the leading edge of fourth-wave feminism, continues the descent of the women's movement into its own parody: the revolution for gender equality that institutionalized inequality.

Latino Empowerment

Gutierrez and Ortega (1991) adapt Gutierrez's (1990) empowerment practice to Latinos (their word) in the United States, assuming that their serious social problems are derived from ethnic oppression. They studied "how group interaction can affect the personal and political levels of empowerment among Latinos" (21). Seventy-three Latino undergraduates at a single university were randomly assigned to a control group or to one of two types of "experimental treatments," that is, group discussions to raise political and social consciousness or to increase ethnic identity. The discussions lasted ninety minutes (the study does not report the number of sessions) with only about 50 percent participation.

> The discussion of Latino identity was primarily positive although at times the discussion took a more negative tone as students related experiences with ethnic stereotyping and discrimination. . . . In the Consciousness Raising group the leaders focused specifically on how Latino status had affected their experiences at the university and on how group efforts for change could be developed and utilized. . . . The overriding goal was to empower the individual on the political level in a collaborative effort. (Gutierrez and Ortega 1991, 30)

The authors found that participants in the consciousness-raising group and the ethnic-identity group were more likely than control participants to express an "interest in participating in activities to improve the status of Latinos" (37). They also found slight increases for the consciousness-raising group in a willingness to consider changes in larger social systems and slight increases for both discussion groups in a willingness to become active on behalf of Latino interests. The authors then extended their findings to empowerment strategies for the larger Latino community.

Gutierrez and Ortega (1991) took the step, rare in the empowerment practice literature, to conduct empirical research of practice. Unfortunately, it cannot sustain its findings or conclusions. The sample of college students is not representative of the Latino community; thus, the extension of the findings to the Latino community is inappropriate. Attrition in participation appears to be high (about 50 percent). There was no effort to protect against experimenter bias, that is, the inducement of supportive responses from participants. More seriously, only attitudes and vague intentions were reported, not actual empowerment activities by subjects, and there was no follow-up to assess whether changes endured. The changes themselves were quite small, while the principal goal to "empower the individual on the political level" was apparently not achieved, as specific political activities of the students were not reported. The consciousness-raising group generally performed better than did the ethnic identity group, which questions whether a strategy of empowerment dedicated to Latinos is necessary. Much similar to the rest of the empowerment practice literature, Gutierrez and Ortega (1991) is a trivial study that demonstrates nothing at all; it is a gesture in support of the field's preferences.[10]

However, the symbolism of Gutierrez and Ortega (1991) worries at the goals of an open democracy.

Gutierrez and Ortega (1991) and Freire (1970, 1973) addressed presumably oppressed Latinos but came up with approaches that differed greatly in mood and tactics while similar in outcomes; that is, both seem to have failed to achieve their goals. They also shared a common purpose—liberation—and the use of the word "empowerment." Still, their crucial differences are undiminished by being largely symbolic.

Their differences in mood, tactics, and strategies uncover different social roles or at least place sectarian empowerment practice in perspective. Freire sought a universal solution to the oppression of a near ubiquitous caste of peasants in Latin America; Gutierrez and Ortega (1991), as one example among many, promote the divisive nationalism of ethnic identity in a multiethnic culture. Freire attempted to break down divisions among those to be empowered in pursuit of universal goals; sectarian empowerment practice does the reverse, creating barriers between the disadvantaged in the United States by imposing ethnicity as the crucial identity. Friere addressed true oppression with revolution; in contrast, Gutierrez addressed imaginary oppression with ersatz change. Freire is a grand statement of discontent, extending the revolutionary and insurrectionist mood to politics on behalf of the truly oppressed; empowerment practice has become a mincing, insipid process that largely divorces individual change from social change in its contentment with a professionally safe process of consciousness raising. Freire never made peace with the oppression of peasants; empowerment practitioners take comfort and professional advance from empty research and ineffective programs.

If failure is inevitable in the face of enduring injustice and unconscionable inequality, then certainly the magnificence of Freire's passionate opposition, taken at considerable risk to himself, is preferable to the inconsequentiality and parochialism of sectarian empowerment practice and the yearning of its practitioners for a safe professional existence. Both may be wrongheaded: Friere's violence engenders greater violence, and his pedagogy seems to ignore the intractability of peasant culture; meanwhile empowerment practice is more effete than seriously targeted on social problems. Still and all, the small influence of professionalized insurrection and empowerment practice may, in fact, be the final judgment by both the oppressed and the so-called "oppressed."

Miscellaneous Empowerment

In addition to the frankly oppressed, the so-called "oppressed," and the somewhat oppressed, empowerment practice has been prescribed to remedy a variety of traditional problems. Judith Lee (2001) attempts to empower the mentally ill through drug therapy and their families with "a warm individualized approach that educates about mental illness, destigmatizes the members' problems, discusses new findings in brain research that offer hope while being realistic. . . ." (272). She demonstrates the virtues of her empowerment approach with case studies but not any systematic evidence of its effectiveness. Her discussion is oblivious of the problems of drug therapy or the serious limitations of community treatment that have been repeatedly documented (Angell 2011a, 2011b, 2011c). Contemporary mental health practice continues to ignore serious evidence that biochemical treatment for "biochemical brain disorders" may actually be harmful and that community treatments continue to have desultory success, if even that. Indeed, if the seriously mentally ill and their families are to be empowered, the costs of care are enormous, greater than hospitalization (Stein and Test 1990; Epstein 2010). As is common after the 1970s, Lee (2001) employs "empowerment" as a synonym for common treatment.

Cochran (in Hurrelmann, Kaufmann, and Losel 1987) sets about empowering working-class and middle-income families in their parenting role through Family Matters, a family support program. One hundred and sixty families were offered the program. One hundred and sixteen families who were not offered the program constituted a control group.

> . . . Two separate approaches were used to involved families in activities related their children. One, a home-visiting approach, was aimed at individual families and made available to all participating families in five of the ten program neighborhoods. Families in the other five neighborhoods were asked to become involved in group activities with clusters of other Family Matters families in their own neighborhoods, in an effort to emphasized mutual support and cooperative action, with family dynamics and the parent-child dyad as the secondary (although explicitly acknowledged) focus. . . . Families were involved with program activities for an average of 26 months, and the program itself came to a close early in the summer prior to first grade entry for most of the target children included in the study. (Cochran 1987)

The results, measured against expectations, were mixed, although Cochran does not provide any quantitative description of outcomes or comparisons with controls. Nonetheless, it appears that many families took advantage of the available services. "However, the most accurate conclusion to be drawn about Family Matters as a program of empowerment is that it was incomplete"; crucially, "it failed to address the question of changing the balance of power between families and controlling institutions" (113). Of even greater concern, Family Matters set out to empower a group that was decidedly not oppressed, although Cochran invokes Freire's definition of empowerment throughout. A less grandiose interpretation sets Family Matters within the context of traditional support services for parents of the mentally ill and, in the end, with customary hit-and-miss outcomes.

Employing one of the rare randomized evaluative designs of empowerment practice, Leung, Tsang, and Dean (2011) assessed the Hands-On Parent Empowerment (HOPE) Program, which was designed to empower parents to "take responsibility for the children's development" (549). The program provided relatively poor immigrant parents in Hong Kong with skills to promote child development; the thirty-session program was conducted by two social workers. The comparison group received six monthly two-hour sessions consisting of information about the parents' roles, self-esteem, behavior management, and the like. The findings of this unusually rigorous evaluation were mixed and modest but "encouraging" in the authors' words. The intervention parents reported less stress for themselves and fewer behavioral problems for their children than did the comparison-group parents. The findings related to social support and self-efficacy were inconsistent, while there was no difference in postintervention child learning scores between the groups. The largest effect sizes were only between 0.4 and 0.5; most were much lower. Apparently none of the changes were reliable.

However, even these modest findings are offset by a number of considerations. The parents were not oppressed; they were migrants within the same culture, spoke the same language, and were doing quite well economically and socially. Attrition was low, suggesting that the parents were highly motivated to participate. Moreover, it stretches the concept of empowerment to encompass parenting skills as a technique of liberation for relatively content, prospering people; from what are they being liberated? Best said, HOPE provided acculturation assistance for eager, grateful migrants making an easy transition within their own culture but was not a program that addressed the needs of the beleaguered.

In an earlier application of HOPE, Leung, Tsang, Dean, and Chow (2009) offered an adaptation of developmental skills programs such as Abecedarian and Head Start to sixteen parents. The program sought "to enhance the learning competence and well being of preschool children from disadvantaged backgrounds through enhancing their parents' skills in supporting their learning" (24). The reported outcomes, including "important insights," were based on the self-reports of program participants. There were no independent, objective measures. However, preschool gains for disadvantaged children seemed to wear off rapidly as is common, and the true test of early interventions lies in prolonged follow-up (Westinghouse Learning Corporation 1969). Moreover, the absence of any comparison group and the small number of highly motivated participants undercuts any conclusion. Empowerment practice is again confused with customary social services that make little, if any, effort to modify social and political structures.

Similarly, Man (1999) reported on rehabilitation for patients suffering from brain injury by employing empowerment as a synonym for self-efficacy and "empowerment status" as an equivalent to progress in recovery. In this sense, all of medical practice is engaged in empowering patients; education is a process of empowering students; street repair is necessary to empower drivers; coaching empowers athletes; and so on until the concept of empowerment has been entirely cleansed of its political and social ambitions.

Tang, Funnell, Brown, and Kurlander (2009) found that empowerment principles were useful in improving the self-management of diabetics; yet the study did not employ a separate control group or follow-up on compliance after the end of the treatment period. Resendez et al. (2000) employed the Vanderbilt Family Project model to empower families caring for their mentally ill children. "The model predicts that increased knowledge, skills and efficacy of mental health services will lead to greater parental involvement and a stronger parent-professional partnership which in turn will produce more positive outcomes for children and families (i.e., increased satisfaction and mental health outcomes" (451). The authors reported that the more empowered a caregiver felt, the more satisfied they were with the services and the more their children improved. Thus, the authors conclude that "family empowerment is a critical component in effective mental health systems" (458). However, as they note, no causal inferences can be drawn from their correlational study. Attrition of subjects and loss of data were not reported except to note that they were ignored in the analyses; thus, self-selection competes with empowerment services to explain the findings. In this way, it is not clear whether feelings of empowerment were the result of the Vanderbilt Family Project services or simply the inherent capacities of some parents, a possibility that cannot be discounted without adequate control groups. The research was also oblivious to possible biases in its data collection: The clinicians measured the outcomes of their own patients; caregiver satisfaction was measured by self-reporting, a procedure that was prone to confuse expressions of gratitude for free services and the kindliness of the clinicians with true estimates of satisfaction. No objective estimates were made of any behaviors. The research demonstrates little at all while it appropriates the concept of empowerment for ancillary mental health care.

Koberg et al. (1999) found that a variety of factors contributed to feelings of empowerment among "technically skilled, professional and managerial hospital employees" (71). The methods are questionable, and the outcomes are suspect. However, this study, among thousands of others, marks the shift in empowerment practice away from the material deprivations of politically and socially marginalized people—the truly needy and powerless—to the subjective perceptions of social elites. Empowerment practice as the pursuit of greater material and political equality has given way in the United States to psychological satisfaction, abandoning revolution and justice for socialization and the efficiency of social institutions.

Similarly, Lecroy (2004) evaluated a twelve-session program to "address developmental tasks critical for healthy psychosocial development such as achieving competent gender identification" (427). The poorly designed study concludes with "encouraging" results and the recommendation for a more rigorous evaluative design. Rather than empowerment, the Go Grrrls (sic) Program is a preventative developmental intervention (but without the capacity to measure prevention). Still, a program that devotes only two didactic sessions to each of six development tasks is unlikely to make much of an impression on adolescents.

Reporting on rehabilitation for patients suffering from brain injury, Man (1999) again employs empowerment as a synonym for self-efficacy and "empowerment status" as an equivalent to progress in recovery. Curiously, the meaning of "empowerment" seems often to simply mean "self-sufficiency" or "self-reliance," which translates easily into social neglect, especially when the interventions are superficial, the positive outcomes (if they occur at all) are transitory, the targets of service are not oppressed but are often poor, and the host cultures are apparently motivated to curb their contributions to need. Through the theater of the perverse, empowerment practice with its little dramas of independence seems to encourage societies to neglect the suffering and grave inequality among their members.

Davey (1998) evaluated a family empowerment program; Mathieu, Gilson, and Ruddy (2006) tested a model for empowering service technician teams; Dunlap (1997) evaluated the effect of cooperative preschool education on family empowerment. Chan, Chan, and Lou (2002) evaluated the empowerment of divorced women in Hong Kong. Bickman et al. (1998) reported mixed outcomes for empowering family caregivers of mental health patients, although they failed to achieve their principal goal, that is, improving the mental health status of the patients; they employed a randomized design, although most of the measures were self-reported by caregivers. Moody, Childs, and Sepples (2003) evaluated an empowerment program to "decrease drug use and strengthen connections to school" of youths; all the data were self-reported by the youths; no control group was employed, and no blood or hair tests were administered to assess actual drug use. Rose and Black (1985) assert the empowerment prowess of case management, day programs, legal advocacy, and organizing without any credible evidence.

Typical both of the appropriation of empowerment for customary health care and of the poor quality of its empowerment research, Frain, Tschopp, and Bishop (2009) concluded that psychological counseling leading to empowerment is an important component of rehabilitation for the disabled. They defined interpersonal empowerment as self-efficacy, self-advocacy, competence, and self-perceived stigma. This reduces to interpersonal assertiveness but has little, if any, demonstrated carryover to political and social activism, the core of empowerment. The authors tested the value of psychological counseling by conducting a web-based survey of people more than eighteen years of age who have a known disability. An unreported number of these people were reached through "disability websites, events and organizations"; of 480 responses, 114 were adequate for the analysis—a response rate of only about 28 percent but probably tiny in consideration of the initial number who were reached. The problem of self-selection by itself, let alone all the unknown but plausible problems of self-report and reliability among largely undefined respondents, should have discouraged the authors from continuing their research. Nonetheless, they persevered to conclude that results of their survey provide "justification for rehabilitation counselors to work on the empowerment of persons with disabilities" (33). In fact, the authors tested nothing at all but the patience of the scientific community in their own field.

Each intervention was inexpensive and short term, even superficial, and employed empowerment to refer to standard social service treatments and standard social service outcomes of increased personal capacity. Still, the studies customarily failed to measure empowerment objectively or its persistence after the end of the program. Each study reported positive, although usually modest, outcomes in the short term but, in each case, the conclusions were invalidated by their inadequate methodologies. Similar poorly supported claims have been made for empowerment practice through an enormous range of social and physical interventions.

Empowerment practice is enamored of Saleebey's strengths perspective that "honors two things: the power of the self to heal and right itself with the help of the environment, and the need for an alliance with the hope that life might really be otherwise" (Saleebey 1996, 303). However, the strengths perspective is, in fact, as vacuous as it seems. Both people and their environment need to be considered in addressing personal and social problems; yet the strengths perspective does not identify how this is to be done. Saleebey summarily dismisses criticisms of the strengths perspective without addressing their seriousness. As its critics claim, the strengths perspective remains "just positive thinking in another guise, simply reframes deficits and misery, is 'Pollyannaish,' [and] . . . ignores or downplays real problems" (Saleebey 1996, 302). Both individual and social problems persist precisely because strengths are inadequate for challenges. More generally, the strengths perspective is typical of the proffered wisdom of the helping professions—a jumble of aphorism, cliché, received wisdom, memory dressed as history, and, lamentably, unquestioned acceptance of social norms parading as self-determination.

Whether practiced within distinctive ethnic, racial, gender, or sexual groups or more broadly among those who share common socioeconomic needs, disability, or even geographic proximity, the outcomes of empowerment remain indeterminate at best, probably ineffective, and possibly harmful. While it is obvious that the status of blacks, women, Hispanics, gays, and others has improved noticeably over the past fifty years, it is not obvious that the changes have been engendered by empowerment practice. Indeed, it may well be that empowerment practice has retarded greater progress by sustaining ideological and political differences among needy groups and by subscribing to the fundamental myths of American romanticism.

Empowerment through Community Organization

Empowerment practice as community organization is more rapture than practice, first with Freire's conscientization; its near contemporary efforts in the 1950s and 1960s at Mobilization for Youth and the War on Poverty's Community Action Program (Epstein 2010); and then later with enthusiasm to build social capital (Putnam 2001) and to eschew conflict through consensus organizing (Gittell and Vidal 1998), among others, and with the defining assumptions of self-sufficiency and self-invention. Freire had little choice, as Brazil's despots were not about to fund their own demise. Yet, modern America always has the option of generosity and social responsibility, which it customarily rejects. Still, each enthusiasm shared the same fate of pursuing the empowerment of the poor and the marginal through ineffective means. Community organization as a professional intervention into troubled groups of people, let alone the dispossessed, has been a failure if the intended outcomes were revolution, increased power, autonomy, or even better problem solving. When not an arrant failure, community organization practice is typically a ceremony that organizes people to affirm popular social values.

"Community organization" is often employed as a synonym for community relations or the outreach activities of a social service agency to its community of support and its service recipients. The activities are evidence of sensitivity to local values and mores, important for any organization, either profit making or not, that depends on the voluntary acceptance of its existence by others. Agricultural extension workers and executives of social services agencies, as examples, are not community organizers but rather people seeking to press a series of ideas within a larger community. Their goal is typically not empowerment per se but rather improvements in efficiency, technology transfer, or the acceptance of particular services. In contrast, agricultural cooperatives and organizations that provide services to their members are probably the result of community organizing efforts.

In this regard, Wagenaar et al. (1999) evaluated a community organization project to reduce alcohol-related problems among young adults. However, their efforts largely involved the dissemination of information of one sort or another "to improve the public health of communities by changing institutional policies, procedures and practices to reduce the flow of alcohol to youth under age 21" (316). Perry et al. (2002) conducted a similar community organization effort to reduce alcohol consumption among adolescents in part through a community organizing effort that "sponsored responsible beverage server training programs, . . . compliance checks in off-sale alcohol outlets, . . . [information dissemination at] community festivals, . . . [and promoting] new policies and ordinances related to teen alcohol use and access to alcohol" (120). Both reported success, and most of their measured outcomes relied on reports by project subjects and participants. At best, both projects employed tactics of aggressive community health outreach to improve the adoption of new program policies. However, neither developed independent community organizations with the goal of addressing socioeconomic inequities, and neither addressed the concerns of marginal or deprived communities.

In addressing similarly modest goals that employ community interventions of one sort or another, Wandersman and Florin (2003) are hard-pressed to enumerate successes, and these are poorly documented. Berkowitz (2001) claims that evidence of successful community coalition building is absent largely because of "methodological obstacles" (213). However, the absence of an ability to evaluate community action should dampen Berkowitz's assurances that successes do, in fact, exist.

When pursued beyond community outreach or community relations, community organization is a planned intervention by trained professionals to improve the self-determination of either a functional community or a geographic community. Its core innovation, to use Rogers' (2003) diffusion theory, is organization itself, the notion that cooperation even among seemingly powerless individuals will further their shared interests through the development of a formal organization that they control. Furthermore, community organization is typically conducted with a community distinguished from the larger community by its needs and its inability to organize itself through the customary, spontaneous politics of the nation. Thus, community organization targets the poor, the disadvantaged, the discriminated, the marginal, and so forth; it presumably would not occur but for the planned intervention of professionals. The political organizer and the community organizer share common techniques, but their purposes, their goals, and their target communities are different, if by no other observation, than that the community organizer is nearly defined by conflict with the majority culture.

Consensus organizing—empowerment without tears—was presumably a serious attempt to develop a practice of community organization that did not rely on conflict (Gittell and Vidal 1998, 2). It was tested in a national demonstration run by the Local Initiatives Support Corporation, a major auspices for community organization in the United States. The project sought to empower poor local communities to pursue better housing and economic development through locally funded and controlled corporations. It selected three target cities for the demonstration. Communities in which an organizing effort had been conducted in recent years were barred from the demonstration, a selection criterion that suggests recognition of the customary failure of community organization and the degree to which it may frustrate local residents through intense participation without much of a payback in successful projects.

The project's specific goals

> were to (1) establish community-based and -controlled community development corporations with neighborhood leaders as board members: (2) foster beneficial financial, technical, and political contacts between residents of targeted neighborhoods and leading organizations and individuals in the support community; and (3) have community development corporations (and community development corporation board members) develop and then demonstrate their competency through the completion of housing development projects. (Gittell and Vidal 1998, 227–28)

After five years, eleven development corporations were still functioning, although none of them had completed successful real-estate programs. Moreover, they had only been able to raise $4.5 million—inadequate for even modest development—most of which was donated by local foundations and public agencies. Apparently, the local financial sector in each city ignored the program, perhaps because it posed neither an opportunity for profit nor a threat to their operation. In addition, resident participation was superficial, and democratic processes were ignored by small controlling cliques.

Nonetheless, the failure did not weaken the organizers' enthusiasm for consensus organizing, its promising capacity for addressing serious material deprivation. A more realistic appraisal would have acknowledged the absence of local resources for physical development in poor communities, not the least because of local complacency. More to the point, the prospect of empowering the poor with vacuous goodwill and without threatening the wealthy seems oblivious to the inadequacy of voluntary and charitable impulses throughout American history.

Putnam (2001) concretized the illusion of the good neighbor as a corporeal presence—social capital—that gave rise to a small industry within the empowerment community. A variety of foundations and private consultant firms set out to market the development of social capital to public officials in beleaguered cities. They promised to address serious problems of neighborhood blight, anomie, crime, and social discord without threats and without even material resources. Social capital, nourished by recognition of the virtues of neighborliness, becomes a bankable resource.

However, despite an enormous run of popularity, social capital has not been transformed into the real thing nor have troubled communities seen the light of affability shining on the true path of self-help. Indeed, both consensus organizing and social capital are current variations in American romanticism, in particular its fantasies of self-help, heroic individualism, localism that is little more than provincial boastfulness, and throughout, a mystical attachment to virtues that defy history and objective reality. Not coincidentally, the parochial agenda of empowerment organizing is largely reserved for the poor and deprived, while the benefits of modernity seem reserved for better situated groups—nostalgia and sentimentality in sustaining American stratification but science and technology as bulwarks of unshared material growth.

It is reasonable and expected that community organization would fail to empower marginal communities through either consciousness raising or self-help. Moreover, there is always the likely danger that community organization by threatening "oppressive" rule will intensify the oppression. This has been the common reaction to protest in many savage states. In more tolerant and open societies, community organization is unlikely to create much of a change, let alone a benefit proportionate to effort, as the conditions of marginal, poor, and otherwise-deprived groups are probably embedded in social priorities. That is, the needy are needy by dint of social priorities but not by some accident of political neglect.

The very logic of community organization, perhaps sensible when communities are small and isolated from each other, is refuted in a society that has specialized almost all of its functions except, paradoxically, the modern nuclear family in which parenting roles are becoming ever more undifferentiated. The attachment of community organization to empowerment as self-reliance may well be self-defeating in a world so dominated by the interdependence of communities that traditional notions of national identity, let alone localism, are barriers to socioeconomic progress. Major social problems—unemployment, education, poverty, environmental pollution, and national security, among others—cannot be resolved within the neighborhood or small community without sufficient resources. Those resources must inevitably be drawn from larger entities and shared equitably to resolve problems and to achieve greater equality and social integration. Even wealthy communities face problems such as unemployment and air pollution that do not originate in them. Consequently, solutions depend on organizational entities that transcend local communities.

The insistence on tactics of consensus deprives the weak of one of their most important tools: conflict. It is also quite disingenuous, as the socially dominant groups that fund community organization rarely shrink from tough competition on behalf of their own interests. In this light, community organization as it is practiced has neutered the initial inspiration of empowerment. Still and all, it is often missed among the more aggressive expressions of community organization and their penchant for theatrical defiance that insurrections of the weak often create disproportionate opposition and may even bait true repression.[11] Thus, community organization of the poor, the deprived, and the marginal—whether pursued through slumped shoulders or fists—is probably doomed in a society that tolerates their deprivations. Put another way, the problems of the deprived customarily develop with the sanction of the society representing a social consensus that is impervious to exhortation.

Community organization's emphasis on local identity cuts against the development of a sophisticated, tolerant, and open society. Localism nurtures a petty "nationalism," a rebarbative sense of righteousness that resists appropriate social learning. Putnam's imagined benefits of neighborliness and LISC's pursuit of social capital as a principal justification for community organization ignore some of the beauties of modern life: the escape from the claustrophobic and intrusive meddling of small town life, personal privacy, the benefits of compartmentalizing existence, and both the economic and intellectual stimulations of the metropolis. Offering the parochialism of community organization to the poor within a globalizing world is about as useful as training them to handle picks and shovels. It is also a cynical diversion of social welfare into a backwater nostalgia that is typically associated with American policy romanticism. Not coincidentally, it justifies ignoring the material needs of the poor and the enormous economic and educational inequalities of American stratification.

Community organization practice devoted to empowerment continues without meeting its own professed goals but persists to perform a ceremonial function. Community organization typically does not engage in conflict with its sources of sanction and support but rather acts to affirm dominant values, notably self-determination as self-help.

Empowerment and Psychotherapy

The initial passions of empowerment practice have settled into complacency, descending from the polemics of Freire and Fanon in behalf of violent political and social revolution to an enchantment with the individual's inner life. Often adopting psychotherapy, contemporary empowerment practice entails verbal exchanges with a professional to explore and change emotions and perceptions through adaptations of cognitive-behavior therapy and even psychodynamic therapy. Consciousness raising has become psychotherapy. It attacks individual passivity—the attitudes of fatalism and self-depreciation, following Friere—as a prod to active political involvement. Unfortunately, it has become the dead end of psychological millenarianism in the pursuit of political and social transformation.

The development of a critical consciousness is the goal of Freire's conscientization, a process of dialogue to empower peasants. "Dialogue creates a critical attitude. It is nourished by love, humility, hope, faith and trust" (Freire 1973, 45). The dialogue between teacher and student appears to be symmetrical with the psychotherapeutic relationship between therapist and patient. The goal in both is to "overcome . . . magic or naïve understanding" (Freire 1973, 46). Indeed, conscientization is similar to cognitive behavior therapy (Beck 1995) in testing reality but with a tacit script of what reality contains. Both assume that appropriate attitudes toward reality will result in appropriate behavior.

Feminist empowerment is often handled frankly as psychotherapy. "The disciplined and skillful use of self disclosure, by the therapist as well as the patient, helps women in the empowerment process which is at the heart of feminist—and all good—therapy" (Greenspan in Howard 1986, 5). "In the therapy session, it is useful to explore and validate experiences of relational empowerment and to help the patient internalize this capacity and learn to establish new relational contexts in which strengths can be affirmed and new growth facilitated" (Surrey in Jordan et al. 1991). Bricker-Jenkins and Hooyman (1986) define feminist practice beginning with consciousness raising and employ the same terms as Freire's conscientization and psychotherapeutic empowerment.

Not surprisingly, even community organization often contains a large psychotherapeutic content, in part through the legacy of Freire's conscientization, but also more directly as a contemporary assault on what it considers attitudes that impede empowerment. Burghardt (1982) addresses both the organizer's "use of self" and the unconscious in organizing psychodynamic processes that draw from Freud, Rogers, and Horney. There is not a hint of agnosticism in his work that often reads as if it were mass-market prescriptions for positive thinking and self-help: "Be modest in your personal goals. . . . Actively use your personal strengths to work on areas of difficulty" (Burghardt 1982, 61).

Empowerment practice and psychotherapy have followed the same trajectory of acquiescence. What began with Freud and the early psychoanalysts as a process of release from the constraints of social custom has become its reverse—a practice of acquiescence to social norms. As Rieff (1966) has observed, the therapeutic has triumphed over the unconventional and the rebellious; the therapeutic has also undermined more substantive and necessarily expensive remedies for the social inequities that justify a concern with empowerment. In a similar transition from release to constraint, empowerment practice through psychotherapy has emerged as its own denial, a conundrum within a fantasy—individual change that does not occur, displacing revolutionary change which cannot succeed.

Both empowerment practice and psychotherapy share the same false assumption that the individual is "self-positing" and, thus, capable of heroic acts to overcome adversity. Contemporary empowerment practice often frames its goals in psychotherapeutic language, becoming satisfied with enhanced ego functioning, self-esteem, attitude change, and the like as evidence of its success. Consciousness raising has largely become the goal rather than an initial step to political change.

Moreover, psychotherapeutic effectiveness is as questionable as the political efficacy of empowerment practice itself.

The march of psychotherapy toward empowerment victory is impeded by three considerations: The potential of rational induction to change attitudes is severely circumscribed by the inability to control the environment of choice; attitude change does not necessary lead to behavior change; and there is little, if any, evidence that psychotherapy has ever been effective against any personal or social problem or has even demonstrated an ability to modify attitudes.

Kahneman (2011) and Piattelli-Palmarini (1994) dampen any enthusiasm for rational choice. Kahneman has repeatedly shown that the context in which a person makes decisions has a profound effect on behavior rather than the attitudes that are brought to the situation. In particular, he largely refuted the notion at the heart of most psychotherapeutic theories that people seek to maximize their presumed best interests. Customarily, therapy attempts to define functional, that is, rational goals for patients and then to modify attitudes, thus freeing the patient from barriers to pursuing those goals.

In corroboration of Kahneman's (2011) skepticism, Chaiklin's (2011) extensive review concluded that there is little evidence that attitude change necessarily precedes behavioral change.

> What stands out in this review on the state of knowledge about the ability of attitudes to predict behavior is that it is murky and not a great deal of progress has been made in clarifying the matter. The one thing that methodological advances have clarified is that attitudes have some utility in predicting behavior when it is not a problem to the person and there is social acceptance of its expression in action. It is not necessary to change attitudes to change behavior. . . . Eighty years of research has done little to improve the ability to predict behavior from attitude. (Chaiklin 2011, 48)

However, the political expression of empowerment—rebelliousness, dissent, conflict, and even economic risk—is often not socially acceptable and does, in fact, pose discomfort or threat to the powerless. What may often seem to be their self-defeating behavior—meekness, acceptance of tyranny, and fatalism—may be adaptive in avoiding persecution, stigma, and social hostility. Liberation through psychotherapy, if more than vaporous euphoria, is still restricted to emotions and largely divorced from behavior. However, if Chaiklin is correct, the emotional rewiring of psychotherapy, when even this occurs, does not predict behavioral change, in this case empowered political and social actions.

The record of psychotherapeutic outcomes provides the most compelling evidence for its ineffectiveness. Psychotherapy has been unable to consistently achieve its behavioral goals and notably those that define empowerment practice. Its clinical literature is more sophisticated than the empowerment literature but so too are its biases and errors. The field's small but persistent critical tradition has been unanswered.[12] The critique centers on the theme that the tests of psychotherapy's effectiveness are impaired and the outcomes are easily reinterpreted as failures. In particular, the voluminous literature related to depression—a condition closely aligned with the feelings of incapacity among the powerless—largely reduces to patients' satisfaction with their therapist, rather than the central question of whether therapy has modified the behaviors associated with depression.

Psychotherapy has not demonstrated a capacity to change any type of false consciousness (a la Marx) whether related to inaccurate perceptions of self or society. Pursuit of empowerment through psychotherapy says much about the paradoxical dominance of the heroic among would-be revolutionaries—transformation by an act of will—in the face of their meek acquiescence to cultural norms. To warn against "hubristic grandiosity" does not prevent it (Simon 1994, 4). The romantic notion of self-invention that defines psychotherapeutic empowerment is, in fact, grandiose, particularly because of the field's consistent failure to empower the powerless.

Empowerment Evaluation

Evaluation itself can apparently empower the oppressed and agencies that seek to liberate them (Secret, Jordan, and Ford 1999). Similar to the older concept of action research,

> empowerment evaluation is the use of evaluation concepts and techniques to foster self-determination. The focus is on helping people help themselves. This evaluation approach focuses on improvement, is collaborative, and requires both quantitative and qualitative methodologies . . . It is a multifaceted approach with many forms, including training, facilitation, advocacy, illumination, and liberation. (Fetterman 1994, 1)

However, self-defined empowerment evaluation research is little different than the more generic attempts to evaluate empowerment practice. Both types deviate from standards of scientific credibility, so much so that all of their findings, undercut by pitfalls of sampling, controls, data reliability, and others, are of little use even for purposes of agency management. Wallerstein and Martinez (1994) provide a qualitative case study of an adolescent substance-abuse prevention program, concluding that "the youth developed an action orientation of caring about the problem, about their own actions, and about each other" (135). These achievements are considered tantamount to empowerment, because they conform with Freire's processes of conscientization, central to his dialogical process of liberation. No data are provided; anecdotes apparently suffice to establish the results. The authors apparently do not see the necessity to describe either the intervention or the sample. Most critically, the research fails to employ a comparison group to track whether, in fact, the treatment lowered substance abuse.

Still, the qualitative case study seems to be the modal methodology of empowerment research. Miller and Campbell (2006) provide a remarkably thorough and devastating review of the genre. Many of their descriptions of the forty-six empowerment research case studies undercut any pretense to liberation practice. The studied programs were targeted on "vulnerable populations" that were not "socially or economically advantaged" (306). Still and all, vulnerability does not constitute oppression. Moreover, "across all cases, community knowledge, organizational learning, and accountability were the principles most evident in descriptions of the cases, and social justice, democracy, and the valuing of evidence-based strategies were the least evident," ". . . a particular irony" for liberation evaluation practice (314). Further, the goals of these evaluations conform to criteria of management efficiency rather than of liberation. Most troubling for the liberationist pretenses of the empowerment research enterprise itself, "although empowerment evaluation advocates for the inclusion of program consumers in the evaluation, and it is they who ultimately are to be empowered, program recipients were seldom part of the empowerment evaluations, relative to what one might expect" (314).

Miller and Campbell's (2006) general comments on the quality of the evaluations vitiate their value as research. Outcomes were frequently asserted but neither empirically measured nor verified. Indeed, the case studies often avoided any empirical measures or reliability checks, relying on "the unique knowledge, experiences and values of the partner community" rather than on "evidence-based practice" (314).

The research was often poorly detailed. A few of the cases actually conformed to all the principles of empowerment evaluation. In short, it is not at all established that "empowerment evaluation actually leads to empowered outcomes" (296).

The situation has not changed subsequent to what it was at the time of Miller and Campbell (2006). A few examples: Gibbs et al. (2009) claim that technical assistance in evaluation will improve the ability of programs, in this case sexual violence programs, to achieve their goals. However, all of the findings are reported by program staff and those who provided the technical assistance. Gibbs et al. (2009) provide no evidence that satisfaction with techniques of collaboration, tailoring of goals, and other assumptions of empowerment evaluation lead to improved program outcomes, let alone credible evaluation. Andrews et al. (2005) recommend "training, role clarity, management of power relations, participant readiness, adequate resources, technology, coaching skill, and mutual support through a coaching network and interagency networks" to empower community-based organizations. However, all the conclusions are impressions of the evaluators who failed to demonstrate that the community-based organizations became more effective as a function of their improved evaluative capacities.

Similarly, insular and subjective evaluative techniques along with deficits in sampling, reliability, and instrumentation undercut Noonan and Gibbs' (2009) discovery of "promising programs to preventing first time perpetration of sexual violence" (55). Expect Respect (Ball, Kerig, and Rosenbluth 2009) was evaluated by group discussion with participants which is an ineffective strategy for reporting the satisfaction of service recipients let alone actual program outcomes. Men Can Stop Rapes—Men of Strength Club and the GaDuGi SafeCenter were not evaluated but simply asserted to be valuable (Hawkins et al. 2009). None of the programs compared their outcomes with control groups of men who did not go through the programs. All of the empowerment evaluations were oblivious of selection bias, that is, the likelihood that these superficial programs attracted groups of men who were unlikely to commit violence against women. Noonan et al. (2009) conclude that these sorts of programs are adopted because of their "fit" with local values but refuse to confront the conflict between these values and empowerment itself. That is, inexpensive programs that preach goodness emphasize individual responsibility and rely on participants to rate their own efforts are compatible with communities unwilling to allocate substantial funds to address serious inequalities or consider that the source of social problems and their remedies lie with expensive and disruptive structural changes. Apparently, empowerment evaluation is often a tool of marketing and program advocacy more than scrutiny and accountability. It is also the virtual contradiction of what empowerment initially intended. Put another way, it is empowering the wrong people, namely those who perpetuate the problem.

Empowerment evaluation assumes that rational techniques merged with anthropological sensitivity—organizational empathy—can assist agencies in achieving empowerment goals.

> Empowerment evaluation has an unambiguous value orientation—it is designed to help people help themselves and improve their programs using a form of self-evaluation and reflection. Program participants conduct their own evaluations and typically act as facilitators; an outside evaluator often serves as a coach or additional facilitator depending on internal program capabilities.... Empowerment evaluation is necessarily a collaborative group activity, not an individual pursuit. An evaluator does not and cannot empower anyone: people empower themselves, often with assistance and coaching. This process is fundamentally democratic. It invites (if not demands) participation, examining issues of concern to the entire community in an open forum. (Fetterman, Kaftarian, and Wandersman 1996, 5)

Shorn of its liberationist grandiosity, empowerment evaluation framed as self-help applies rational techniques to organizational management. Unfortunately, it labors under the burden of its ideological commitments—"its unambiguous value orientation"—that insist on its plausibility. This blind faith in empowerment evaluation may explain why so many of its applications are biased, subjective, and distorted.

Under the best of circumstances, empowerment evaluation ignores the degree to which rational information is not compelling for practitioners and agencies that enjoy a convenient entente with contemporary social preferences. Moreover, self-help is a fiction and an exhausting dead end in the common situation in which change requires resources that poor people and the needy lack. For the most part, empowerment evaluation, in the manner of empowerment practice, fulfills a ceremonial role in affirming social values—heroic individualism and self-help—rather than a production function in actually improving the conditions of the beleaguered by the provision of resources, including power. Indeed, empowerment evaluations have failed to produce demonstrable improvements in services, in the administration of empowerment agencies, or in social conditions.

Establishing Effective Outcomes

Not only empowerment evaluation but also the general evaluative literature of empowerment practice is deeply flawed. It has not matured in its fifty years of existence, continuing to rely on collaborative case studies that patronize the needy and methodologies which parody science.

Even the most comprehensive reviews of the field and its attempts to develop theories of practice largely ignore the problem of effectiveness and the quality of information. Indeed, both the textbooks of empowerment practice and the conceptual papers read like theological tracts that test the consistency of articles of faith by plumbing founding documents and original meanings. Barbara Simon's (1994) *The Empowerment Tradition in American Social Work* considers practice to be a "school of democracy" but never evaluates the outcomes. She covers hundreds of years of empowerment programs without speaking to their effects, only their intentions. Tacitly then, Simon's history promotes the ceremonial function of empowerment practice as a bulwark against paternalism but without concern for its professed material aims.

In another prominent example, Hur (2006) attempts to develop a typology of the processes of empowerment but in an extensive discussion of its stages across many fields, it fails to separate the effective from the ineffective. Apparently, Hur's (2006) only inclusion criteria for relevant literature requires that a candidate study attend to theory and contain "ideas for the empowerment process and its cognitive elements" (523). In the end, Hur comes up with an empowerment process that seems the equivalent of the generic process for communicating innovations (Rogers 2003) which simply standardizes the common understanding of how change occurs (Lapiere 1965).

Hur (2006) drew conclusions from problematic material that deserved a castigating analysis more than naïve belief. Indeed, none of Hur's base of research can sustain the leap from weak evidence to grand conclusions. Foster-Fishman et al. (1998) go from a "constructivitist" case study of forty-nine employees in a single human service agency to broad conclusions about "the assumptions underlying empowerment

61

theory" (527), the appropriateness of developing "a global measure of empowerment" (528), and "implications for the design of empowerment interventions" (530).

From a total of fourteen interviews conducted across three cities, Ibanez et al. (2003) draw "theoretical and practical implications for future disaster research in developing countries" (1). Broughton et al. (2004) reach conclusions about emancipatory change in community health on the basis of a five-year demonstration in cancer prevention that reports on neither the actual degree of cancer prevention nor its correlates such as smoking abatement. Similarly, Peterson and Reid (2003) report that participants in substance-abuse prevention activities felt empowered, but they fail to report on the success of those activities and whether feelings of empowerment actually led to empowerment. Bellamy and Mowbray (1998) reach conclusions about supported education and empowerment for the mentally ill on the basis of two focus group sessions.

Gist (1987), Moreau (1990), Chronister (2003), Carr (2003), and Zeldin (2004) spare hardly any word from their encomiums of empowerment theory for the issue of effectiveness and credible information. The remaining research cited by Hur (2006) is trivial, irrelevant, poorly executed, or some combination of these faults (Secret, Jordan and Ford 1999; Itzhaky and York 2000; Angelique, Reischl, and Davidson 2002; Boehm and Staples 2002; Boehm and Staples 2004; Boydell and Volpe 2004; Diversi and Mecham 2005).

Empowerment practice has graduated into the platitudes of textbook assurances that are often supported with even less systematic evidence than Hur (2006) relied on. The textbooks customarily share a common rhetoric, first invoking the oppression of those in need as a justification for empowerment practice, then detailing its characteristics, outlining its applicability, and finally adding a few words on evaluation. The textbooks are more ideological than clinical, relying on unquestioned touchstones of belief—participation, Saleebey's (1996) "strengths perspective," self-reliance, and self-help, as examples—to fill in for missing evidence of effectiveness. They customarily appeal to the founding empowerment literature (e.g., Freire 1970, 1973; Gutierrez 1990) as though it offers compelling evidence of effectiveness, and they then cite additional research that is uniformly flawed.

The textbooks typically sidestep the weakness of the research, in part by endorsing empowerment evaluation as a contribution to the process of empowering people through enhanced participation, but usually by simply ignoring the lack of credible information. Simmons and Parsons (in Allen-Meares and Garvin 2000) only acknowledge problems with research in a single phrase that is quickly contradicted by their appreciation for the research: "Although this research is limited, it has been most useful in our efforts to explain and test empowerment practice" (118). Just this sort of malleability allows Lee (2001) to assert the effectiveness of empowerment for the mentally ill and their families based only on weak case studies. Similarly, the textbooks of practice and their primary literature as well typically inflate modest and often transitory improvements, such as in-skills training for the activities of daily living, to sustain the plausibility of liberationist ambitions.

Empowerment practice itself seems to have become coextensive with professional helping; empowerment is customarily assumed as the goal of helping that converts all helping processes into empowerment practice. Empowerment practice, liberation, and oppression perfuse even those practice texts that are not devoted to empowerment practice per se. Gitterman and Germain's (2008) description of empowerment could easily apply to the rest of their "life model" interventions. Without ever mentioning empowerment, *Ethnicity and Family Therapy* justifies practice devoted to separate ethnic groups on grounds of distinct group cultures (McGoldrick, Giordan and Garcia-Preto 2005) but with as little success as Solomon (1976). Its goals for therapy are the same as those for empowerment practice with the seriously mentally ill, and its evidence for effectiveness is similarly weak.

The great expansion of the use of the empowerment idiom between the second and third editions of Seabury, Seabury, and Garvin (2011), for instance, follows the increased popularity of empowerment practice in the helping professions. In fact, "there is debate over whether the empowerment strategy is a new paradigm for practice or just a new term for labeling the core values and beliefs that have always been part of social work," which suggests that the deficits of empowerment practice also hobble social work and the other helping professions (Sheafor and Horejsi p 2003, 416).[13]

There is little difference, if any, between the empowerment process and the customary helping process: Both rest on the assumptions that personal change is possible and can be facilitated through professional interventions; both believe in self-determination, the dignity of the individual, and the importance of self-respect; both emphasize self-awareness and broader understanding of the environmental causes of individual problems; both encourage initiative; and social work, counseling, clinical psychology, pastoral counseling, and the rest of the helping professions share the belief that "empowerment, as an overall strategy and guiding philosophy, is applicable in work with all clients and in all settings" (Sheafor and Horejsi 2003, 418). Indeed, both empowerment practice and helping practice share similarly weak research and lack credible support for their assumptions or systematic evidence of their effectiveness.

The sly self-deception that allows social work to refer to service recipients as clients belies empowerment itself by masking the fact that few service recipients exert much control in the helping relationship or even participate voluntarily. Poor and needy service recipients enter the process of empowerment and helping without the consumer's control as clients who can fire their lawyers, plumbers, and hair-dressers or who can walk away when dissatisfied. They customarily come to professionals in search of money, food, housing, jobs, and so forth or because they have been ordered there by the courts or welfare departments under the threat of serious sanctions for noncompliance.

In short, empowerment practice has proceeded from theory to application without the inconvenience and expense of testing. A more critical interpretation would remark on its retreat from social service accountability to ideological safety and social acceptability. Empowerment research and empowerment evaluation are more pretentious and biased than scientific, usually little more than the authors' self-serving diary notes. The field's primary studies seem to take permission from the noble quest of liberating the oppressed to violate nearly every canon of credible research. Empowerment research is an intransigent rejection of objective reality for a more compliant, postmodern existence in which reality is replaced by wishfulness and convenience. Sometimes, an absence does prove a presence. The fact of so few evaluations of empowerment practice and the poor quality of the few attempts to measure outcomes suggests that recipients, practitioners, and the culture itself are quite satisfied. Few seem to have any stake in its effectiveness. In the end then, without a production function, empowerment practice is left with only symbolic meaning but for obedience, adaptation, self-reliance, and conformity rather than rebellion and liberation.

Notes

1.   The present work evaluates attempts to establish the outcomes of empowerment practice against standard rules of social science evidence.

The randomized controlled trial, that is classical designs, has long been the gold standard for establishing the outcomes of interventions even in social work and the helping professions. However, the application of randomized controlled design is often impeded by practical, ethical, and cost barriers. These difficulties are not warrants for weaker designs that undercut the authority of research to the extent to which they deviate from credible methods. Empowerment practice, more often than not a clinical intervention—centralized and handling individuals—cannot fall back on the customary excuses to justify its porous research, often qualitative case methods, and even less credible designs. Clinical practice is the most convenient setting for randomized designs. The problem of applying credible methods to empowerment practice is rarely one of conceptual clarity. Once a program selects its goals, that is, the outcomes of its interventions that define empowerment, it would seem to be obliged to measure effectiveness, a duty both to scholarly probity and to the powerless, which may be the same thing. The utility of randomized designs are appreciated even in third-world development (see the work of Esther Duflo, although it received only minimal attention in the 2005 World Bank report Narayan D. (ed.), *Measuring Empowerment: Cross-Disciplinary Perspectives* [Washington, DC: The World Bank]). In fact, the report looks more similar to a catalog of the problem than its solution. No scientifically credible outcome studies emerged from the searches to testify to the effectiveness of any form of empowerment practice. The monotony of weak research is only sampled in this work. Yet, the conclusions of this analysis are weakened to the extent to which its bibliographic searches are incomplete, and credible programmatic outcomes exist to sustain the effectiveness of empowerment practice.

2. Wilson unleashed an enormous controversy, substantionally more than 1,000 commentaries and citations of *The Declining Significance of Race* in the few years after its publication. Resistance to the notion was not only notable in the black intellectual community (e.g., Edwards 1979; Jennings 1979; Pettigrew 1979) but also prominent in sociology, political science, and law (e.g., Bentley 1978; Omi 1980; Shulman 1981; Thomas 1993; Morris 1996). There was also considerable support (Sundquist 1978; Sakamota and Tzeng 1999). Whatever deficit may have existed in Wilson's methods, time has validated the decline of racism in explaining American inequality. Much of the commentary surrounding the book attempted objective analyses. However, the critics' analyses, by and large, have the same limitations as those of Wilson. Nonetheless, the criticisms of Wilson may say much about professional and social stakes and little about the value of his book.

3. Among others, Juan Williams' (2006) *Enough* was written in support of Bill Cosby's excoriation of blacks who fail. It continues a persistent theme of personal responsibility within the black intellectual community.

4. The few program evaluations subsequent to Gutierrez (1990) only address separate groups of women of color and are handled elsewhere in the analysis. No empowerment program apparently handled mixed groups of women. The Thomson Reuters citation indexes only produced twenty-nine hits for the combination of "women of color" and "empowerment." Very few were program evaluations.

5.   There are many thoughtful works that place feminism within a complex social context, but even these works customarily return to a romanticism of heroic overcoming in addressing barriers to women's goals. As examples, Echols (1989); Bush (1992); and Brenner (2000). The appetite for the romantic was prominent in the inspiring second-wave feminist books, notably Friedan's (1963) *The Feminine Mystique*.

6.   Seventeen additional outcome studies claimed to empower women. All of them offered standard health interventions usually involving nursing and health education. To encompass standard health promotion and education of one sort or another—neonatal care, AIDS prevention and treatment, cardiac self-care, and so forth—within the definition of empowerment practice distorts its essential meaning by ignoring political and social activism. Better said, these studies appropriate a stylish word to enhance standard practice that has few, if any, direct social and political implications. See, as examples, Butckhardt, Clark, O'Reilly, and Bennett (1997); Larsen, Oldeide, and Malterud (1997); Mein and Winkleby (1998); and Mishra et al. (1998). Moreover, the review of outcome studies of women's empowerment practice did not identify a single substantial evaluation. Those reported in the body of the manuscript are among the best of a very deficient lot, attesting to the observation that the heart of the women's movement lies in political and social activity and not in the treatments of empowerment. It also sustains the observation that the women's movement is largely unconcerned with issues of caste and class.

7.   Markward and Yegidis (2010) correctly observe that neither Van den Bergh (1995) nor Peterson and Lieberman (2001) "provides empirical data on assessing and treating the mental health disorders that are typical among economically disadvantaged women" (xi). They might also have included Howard (1986), among others, in their criticism. However, Markward and Yegidis (2010) hardly repair the problem by citing clinical studies uncritically. Indeed, none or their recommended mental health interventions survive an analysis of their methods; none provide scientifically credible evidence of successful treatment. The absence of credible evidence-based practice in mental health is handled later in the section "Empowerment and Psychotherapy," specifically in Epstein (2006); Throop (2009); and Moloney (forthcoming).

8.   Bush (1992) questions the effectiveness of the women's movement to achieve empowerment; its interim demands, often for social services or for changes in the judicial system, become institutionalized and co-opted the initial fervor for more thoroughgoing change. Bush addresses reforms that are concerned with violence against women. However, the quality of the evaluations of these services is typically too unsophisticated to establish any effect. In addition to studies addressed earlier, see Maciak et al.'s (1999) evaluation of a program to prevent violence against Latina's (why not all women or people in general?) and D'Haene's (1995) evaluation of a feminist-based adolescent group therapy program. The poor attention to outcomes again draws attention to the indifference of the women's movement to poorer members of the sisterhood.

9.   The same analysis would seem to cover the gay liberation movement in the United States. It pursues socioeconomic equality for gays in the terms of

American stratification. Its special interest in AIDS research and treatment is a communal priority rather than a pursuit of broader social fairness that might be expressed in generous care and treatment of all chronic disease patients. As with the women's movement, the success of the gay rights movement is explained by the modesty of its goals, which remain largely procedural rather than substantive.

10. The literature on Latino empowerment is rather small, most within the health and mental health fields where it largely handles traditional service issues (see as one example, Carballo-Dieguez 2007). A few studies attempt to handle empowerment reports on trivial services and to evaluate them both poorly and protectively (see, as examples, Barreto 2007; Lopez 2008; Berg et al. 2009; Garcia-Reid and Reid 2009; Maciak et al. 2009).

11. Piven and Cloward's (1971) argument that an insurrection of the poor would inevitably create accommodation was profoundly undercut by Dodenhoff's (1998) analysis. On its face, the notion of small weak minorities challenging embedded cultural preferences would seem to be futile. Piven and Cloward are as much in the romantic tradition as the culture itself, with both insisting on the heroic possibilities of the committed will.

12. Some of psychotherapy's critics: Gross (1978); Zilbergeld (1983); Epstein (1995, 2006); Dineen (1996); Eisner (2000); Smail (2005); and a few others. Despite their lethal observations, many critics still maintain a loyalty to the field, arguing that some portion of practice is, in fact, effective; for example, Zilbergeld and anxiety, even without adducing credible research to sustain their fading hopes. Psychotherapy's broad popularity pays tribute to its ceremonial function in affirming the nation's faith in extreme individualism. The fact that it is pseudoscience rather than a pragmatic clinical practice is an aside to its persistence as ritual.

13. The social work textbooks are repetitive and obedient to empowerment practice in fact, if not in name. They are published by prestigious university presses and frankly commercial ones, all seeking to make a profit from the college market by riding the pulse of educational fashion but without much effort at critical analysis. Most of the recent textbooks contain shiny covers, colorful graphs and photos, insets, bulleted sections, indentations, student exercises, and historical sections; they cost a fortune but are not worth a fraction of their price. See as additional examples: Reamer (1994); Johnson (1995); Zastrow (2004); Kirst-Ashman and Hull (2012); and Shulman (2012).

A Knowing Misadventure

Contemporary empowerment practice in the United States is a vestige of the revolutionary impulse to free the world's oppressed and a remnant of the nation's mass movements for greater socioeconomic equality. While professing goals of social and political transformation, empowerment practice is most often realized as a clinical intervention whose core techniques are frequently psychotherapeutic. Consistent with the nation's refusal to remedy the inequalities of American economic stratification, empowerment practice typically pursues a tame transformative, psychic millenarianism that abides national values.

American reform movements have unfortunately traded off between inclusion on the one hand and decency, equality, and adequacy on the other. The compromises defer to the aspirations of mobile blacks, Latinos, women, gays, and so forth, providing access to the prevailing American system but without remedying broad inequalities. The modest demands of the nation's reform movements have accommodated political reality in achieving successes that are customarily more procedural than substantive. Affirmative Action policies, a prime example, have largely benefited better-educated white women and relatively few well-educated minorities; they pose little threat to American stratification compared with policies that redress poverty, provide universal access to quality education and jobs, establish a public preschool and day-care system, assure universal health coverage, and so forth.

Empowerment practice has been constructed on a series of dubious assumptions: that attitude change precedes behavior change; that needy groups in the United States are oppressed; that the needy share empowerment's notions of their suffering and, thus, are motivated to seek liberation; that their presumably false consciousness is amenable to reeducation; that the empowerment of minority groups is feasible through sectarian empowerment practice; and that sectarian strategies are consistent with the universal values and goals of the field's revolutionary inspirations.

The fallacies at the heart of empowerment practice—in their own way, tributes to Kahneman's cognitive distortions—are coincidental with American policy romanticism, its reliance on an extreme individualism—the omnipotence of will—and, thus, personal agency. Personal agency extends to individual responsibility for both success and failure and, thus, endorses the fairness of American stratification. The tenets of policy romanticism are the widely shared conservative preferences, intensified over the past decades, of the American people.

Nevertheless, empowerment practice has never demonstrated any ability to achieve even its modest psychological goals, let alone any of its revolutionary pretences. There is no scientifically credible evidence that any form of empowerment practice has benefited, let alone empowered, the poor, the oppressed, the needy, or others in distress. For that matter, there is no credible evidence that empowerment practice has achieved psychological fulfillment in liberating less beleaguered people from their demons. On its part, empowerment evaluation is neither credible evaluation nor effective empowerment practice but rather a conceit of postmodern narcissism. The field's refusal to employ credible science—indeed, its frequent hostility to objectivity and coherence—places empowerment practice alongside alternative medical procedures such as acupuncture; faith healing; herbal remedies; and the frank superstitions of reading palms, tea leaves, and tarot cards to predict the future. Indeed, Madame Blavatsky's Theosophy and Mary Baker Eddy's Christian Science occupied in their time the same role as contemporary empowerment practice by affirming prevailing social preferences. Empowerment practice persists as a ceremony of American values, a church of civic priorities with a stormy rhetoric of liberation but a reality of exhortation to salvation through personal adaptation.

Social change is not a process of heroic overcoming, despite the ubiquitous industry that fuels popular demands for saints, miracles of God's favor, and national chosenness. Social change occurs through more mundane political processes as large constituencies perceive their common interests in reformed institutional arrangements that are customarily engendered by economic innovation that is neither controlled nor socialized (LaPiere 1963; Rogers 2003). In this way, the political empowerment of the subjugated, disadvantaged, marginalized, and needy proceeds from mass movements that are generated more by changing economic imperatives and long-standing grievances than by planned insurrection.

The fact that mass movements inevitably develop leadership and organizational structure promotes the romantic illusion of heroic overcoming that power was developed largely as an act of will—the Olympian perseverance, irresistible charisma, and spellbinding oratory of individual actors—in triumph over oppressive conditions. It obscures the underlying forces that impel natural adaptations to new circumstances. The influence of leadership and planned change is commonly as exaggerated as empowerment practice's barren promises of transformation. Indeed, the compelling social effects of changing economic conditions—from the industrial revolution itself to more recent transformations in production—have probably exerted a larger influence in molding social institutions than any form of consciousness raising, psychotherapy, or even formal education. In just this way, improvements in the conditions of equality of blacks, Latinos, women, gays, and others proceeded from mass movements, specifically the civil rights movement, the women's liberation movement, and the gay empowerment movement, which themselves took strength from the broader social permission to acknowledge the momentum of changed conditions. Empowerment practice is a theatrical remnant of those struggles, and their large, unfinished agendas—the enormous amount of prevailing deprivation in the United States—measure their very modest success.

Empowerment practice consists of professionalized forms, that is, the routinized accommodations, compromises, and even the rituals of the mass reform movements. It embodies their armistice agreements with the dominant society and the new normative consensus; empowerment practice institutionalizes prevailing norms as a statement of what the culture has come to consider the conditions of empowerment. Thus, empowerment practice separately dedicated to blacks, Latinos, women, gays, the impoverished, and others lays out the battle plan to empower those not immediately benefited by the mass movements themselves. Whatever benefits accrued to those in need date to the success of mass movements rather than from empowerment practice itself, the mementos of those movements, and the reliquary of their revolutionary hopes.

The ineffectiveness of empowerment practice is paradoxical in the face of its large and growing popularity. Logically, a practice that does not achieve its goals (in this case, liberation and empowerment) should end as its auspices seek more effective interventions. The paradox of empowerment practice is deepened with the observation that it is

71

largely funded and sanctioned by the very entities that are presumably the barriers to liberation and the objects of revolution—the very governments that are presumably the agents of the oppressive society. The paradox is resolved by dispelling one of the field's heroic fallacies: empowerment practice is not autonomous. It does not invent itself. Empowerment practice is a social institution that is quite obedient in spite of its revolutionary pretensions. In this sense, the evaluation of clinical outcomes is irrelevant to a practice of ideological reinforcement.

The field's complacency with its failures and often its refusal to confront them begins to suggest a social accommodation that documents the conversion of a production function in social change into a ceremony that affirms social norms. Empowerment practice typically does not evaluate itself nor does it allow others to do so. Its few evaluations are more memoirist reportage than objective and coherent outcome assessments. The field acts as though its truths and virtues are manifest—from the lips of God to the ears of the Higher Power wing of the helping professions. Empowerment practice does not learn from its failures; it abides its little dramas of insurrection as a self-pitying Sisyphus, but it moves no rock. Empowerment practice seems indifferent to its reality, a willful ignorance that is socially useful and contradicts one of its own metaphysical assurances that attitude change precedes behavior change. In fact, the behavior of empowerment practice has changed radically over the past few decades with little change in its attitudes.

The concept of empowerment has been vulgarized, coming to refer to usual improvements in individual functioning, thus encouraging social work as well as nursing, rehabilitation medicine, and many other fields to claim that they pursue political and social change by simply going about their daily chores without actually measuring empowerment outcomes. Improvements in the activities of daily living, socialization, psychological coping, and physical rehabilitation are not what Freire, Fanon, King, Freidan, and their contemporaries had in mind when they pressed for the empowerment of deprived people. Indeed, what began as an impulse for social change based on broad social responsibility and universal values of decency has grown into its very opposite—an affirmation of self-sufficiency, personal responsibility, and sectarian preeminence. A culture that refuses to accept social responsibility for the welfare of its citizens embraces empowerment practice to endorse its prevailing preference for the needy to take responsibility for themselves.

Christened by the radical left, empowerment practice has drifted to the insipid center, popular to all, offensive to none. It is as devoid of substance as the contemporary rhetoric of the American Revolution and its founding myths. Empowerment practice incorporates a faint-hearted structuralism, often muttering about the misfortunes of others from the secure precincts of tenured academia. Irony does not capture the strangeness of a contemporary empowerment movement that actually stands for the opposite of its inspiration.

Its frequent dedication to an exclusive sectarian practice for blacks, Latinos, women, or others resurrects tribal boundaries in denial of a national consciousness that is concerned with broad need. Its strategy of compensatory bigotry fails at revolution but succeeds in strengthening a muted but ever-present theme of American society that those in need are normal primitives who should, in fact, be isolated from the dominant culture (Swigert and Farrell 1977). Where empowerment practice may segregate service recipients with good although misguided intentions, the society interprets their separateness as a confirmation of baseness and, thus, their ineligibility for warmer, more generous regard. Rather than the revolutionary heroes of their fantasies, contemporary empowerment intellectuals, "vulgar opportunists" following Fanon, are tame, verbal, and tribal rather than violent and national. The empowerment of Freire and Fanon, a radical assault on structural oppression, has largely degenerated into talk therapy in one form or another that is neither effective nor politically transformative. Freire and Fanon had a compelling grasp of the problem if not of the solution. Their epigones have neither. Still, the entire tradition of empowerment practice shares a common experience: empty programs that fail to achieve their goals.

The segregation of empowerment practice by race, gender, ethnicity, and so forth resurrects the bleakest chapters in American history. It employs the same processes of demonization, stereotypy, and scapegoating that presumably cause oppression to counter it. By imagining definitive subcultural characteristics of ethnicity, race, and gender that justify separate paths to liberation, it rejects the rigors of objectivity and the concrete and forgets the painful ascriptions of inferiority that for centuries condoned the imposition of de jure and de facto apartheid on American citizens and deprived women of common civil rights. "Separate" and "equal" are not one and the same. The intellectual processes that sanction separate treatment are as troubling as their effects. The intense subjectivity of empowerment practice and the self-certifying belief in manifest virtue that excuse it from common accountability exert rebarbative influences on democratic policy making. In many cases, empowerment practice promulgates myths of martyrdom and rites of passage through the sanctification of suffering. These myths and rites embody the same confusion of Providence as virtue that lies at the heart of American stratification. Empowerment practice remains a form of pietism, although bounded in its expression by the conventions of scholarly discourse. Nothing returns the wandering civic imagination to self-protective aggrandizing quicker than indulging itself with tests of godliness and rituals of purification that it applies to others. Empowerment practice is a callous society's ritualistic degradation of those in need.

Empowerment Practice and Policy Romanticism

Empowerment practice is an expression of policy romanticism. It refers to the embedded social beliefs that sustain romantic social policy. The notion draws from both continental philosophy and literary romanticism, but it is inferred from the consistency of political and social choice and describes the underlying beliefs that constitute a social commitment to the romantic. Policy romanticism embraces the core beliefs of democratic populism in the United States. Prevailing over democratic progressivism and its commitment to pragmatism in social policy making, democratic populism and its flight from reason have dominated political traditions in the United States.

Policy romanticism in the United States is defined by an exaggerated individualism that imposes heroic expectations for personal responsibility, by a sense of personal election and national chosenness, which lies at the heart of American exceptionalism, and by truth derived from personal intuition rather than from objective tests. It expresses itself in a series of distorted beliefs about society and individuals that are deeply held and relatively permanent institutions of the culture and is seemingly impervious to the challenges of evidence. Extreme individualism and the sense of exceptionalism persist, because they are accepted as self-evident, manifest truths. The gnomic certitudes of the American creed are consistent with its preference for pietistic religion and the pervasive superstition and magical thinking of American culture. The fact that the literature of empowerment practice is so devoid of scientific rigor, let alone simple objective coherence, is an extension of its social role as an incantation of American belief. It need not prove itself beyond dogma and doctrine. Indeed, the true belief of its literature is an iteration of the true belief of American exceptionalism that is certified by epiphanies—"spontaneous intuitions" following Piattelli-Palmarini (1994)—rather than proof.

The distortions of policy romanticism are the "inevitable" extensions of the cognitive illusions which are coincidental with the social preferences that engender American priorities and their socioeconomic stratification. Policy romanticism is a flight from reason and reality, and empowerment practice is one of its expressions. Empowerment practice both as insurrection and as hypocrisy extends the romantic tradition of extreme individualism and heroic overcoming.

The radical program is as romantic as its vulgarization in empowerment practice. Freire and Fanon assumed that a revolutionary will was a fearsome near ineluctable force, that the oppressed could be mobilized to confront their own conditions on a march to transform the systems which oppressed them, and that enlightenment would proceed in predictable directions to achieve a more egalitarian society. They also seemed to assume a historical imperative toward revolutionary ends, a natural progress of history to transformative democracy and individual self-determination.

Neither Freire nor Fanon confronted the contradictions of revolutionary governments in control or the fact that many poor and oppressed illiterates are loyal to their constraining cultures. For all of their injunctions to deal with reality, Freire in particular but the revolutionary tradition in general invoked the central romantic theme that reality is a product of self-invention and that a revolutionary will could create a preferable reality. However, the empowerment revolutionaries themselves lacked the will to confront oppression by the masses, the frequency that destruction and hatred become embedded by broad consent, and the courage to apply a critical consciousness to its near-uniform failures.

The insistence on the power of the revolutionary consciousness coincides with Fichte's self-positing ego and the tradition of self-invention. Revolutionary theories have characteristically propagated the notion that the cadres of change could resocialize themselves and others to the promised utopia through a variety of inspired techniques. Unfortunately, those techniques were often cruel in the case of the totalitarian governments or inane in the hands of the helping professions. None of them were clever enough to copy the Norwegians, who send their winter blues-afflicted citizens to sunny climes by way of helping them maintain their fervid commitment to the Norwegian way of life.

Oppression itself is perhaps the founding distortion of contemporary empowerment practice in the United States. It has been employed to defend the sectarian nature of much of empowerment practice—special programs for blacks, women, Hispanics, and such. However, sectarian practice based on unique subcultural qualities and the desirability of preserving them recalls the romantic notions of immanence at the core of American bigotry. Cultural diversity is a convenience of American preferences reducing pressures for greater equality by enshrining inequality as subcultural respect. Still, even when suffering injustices and inequalities, American citizens rarely conform to notions of the politically and socially oppressed. To apply oppression and, thus, liberation to American society is hyperbolic and isolates empowerment practice from relevance to contemporary problems and needed reforms. In fact, empowerment practice performs a ceremonial role of social restraint, adaptation, and conformity rather than change.

Oppression in the literature of empowerment practice, both its clinical forms and often its earlier revolutionary expression, seems more a romantic flight of fancy, even a sense of the soul's enchainment, rather than a concrete fact of political terror and social depravity. Much of the psychotherapy of liberation recalls the more traditional mood of literary romanticism, its lassitude, and otherworldliness. Indeed, the yearning of empowerment practice for psychic liberation opens itself to criticisms of narcissism as it becomes deeply introspective, intuitive, and self-certifying in its liberationist pretensions rather than socially and politically activist.

Sentimentality in social welfare policy and the helping professions is a triumph over reality that soothes the accommodation with dominant social preferences, confusing the myths of concern and caring with authentic service. The distorted notion of oppression buttresses the field's self-righteousness that gives it permission to ignore accountability and to maintain an exclusionary sectarian approach to the provision of a social service. The oppression that justifies empowerment practice is a creation of the field, an imaginary condition, which perversely has worked out to the detriment of those in need and not least by isolating them from acceptance in the dominant culture and, thus, a more generous public provision for their needs.

The romantic assumptions of contemporary empowerment practice that endorse its promise to liberate the oppressed are no less fanciful. The individual is not the hero of empowerment illusion but a weak element in a fearsomely influential society—a reed in a windstorm—that largely determines its members' fates. Serious personal and social problems have not been amenable to exhortation or the thin provisions of the social services. On its part, psychotherapy of one sort or another has not achieved empowerment. Rather, the experience of psychotherapy and interventions of talk and exhortation generally refute the ability of people to employ reasoning to change emotions, persona, and character. Empowerment practice is the triumph of emotion over reason. It is not serious clinical practice but rather a repository of romantic ideology, ritualistically repetitive and mystically certain of the virtues of extreme individualism, personal responsibility, and chosenness; that is, the entitlement of America to its claims on citizen loyalty. Articles of faith transcend evaluation but "sooner or later every romanticism demands ... the sacrifice of the intellect" (Baeck 1970, 207).

It is no surprise that liberation fails; it is an unlikely pursuit whose achievement is largely restricted to mystics, psychotics, and those who can afford to purchase a life of comfortable illusion. The arc that empowerment practice traveled from political insurrection to individual treatment is traced by the appeasement of popular values. Neither strategy has been effective; in fact, both achieved their ideals with the same frequency as transmigrating souls, sleep learning, and extrasensory perception. Rather than transformative enterprises, the practice of political revolution and the practice of the social clinic are only affirming ceremonies of political and social moods. The shift to treatment is not pacification itself but rather evidence that dissent has already been socialized into prevailing grievance procedures and fitted to the nation's romantic preferences. The conciliation of the helping professions despite their intellectual weaknesses is less a moral issue—freedom of action has never been the realm of social institutions—than a cultural event. The adaptation of the insurrectionist mood to embedded, determinative social preferences defines political reality. In this way, the analysis of social welfare becomes a cultural critique, and the failure of empowerment practice pays tribute to the resiliency of inequality in the United States.

There are terrible iniquities in the world, and many people have been truly oppressed in many nations. Their liberation from tyranny is estimable and humane, and violence is often a necessary recourse. Yet, empowerment practice does not soften their plight, and the confusion of goals and practice throughout its literature obscures the weaknesses that impede measurable progress. Fields such as social work, psychotherapy, community counseling, community development and community organization, nursing, management, public administration, and others incorporate empowerment practice as points of faith in posturing their deep, deep commitments to those in need. Indeed, empowerment practice actually perpetuates those needs by falsely promising cheap solutions to embedded social inequities, as though self-help, self-realization, self-actualization, and the will of the poor were sufficient to achieve liberation. In just this way, the ever-obedient helping professions proselytize heroic individualism and the romantic notion of self-invention through their interventions. Their devotion to individual change, ceremonialized in empowerment practice, supplants more material attempts to resolve inequality.

Real and Imaginary Oppression

The justification for empowerment is impeded by nostalgia for suffering, that is, an invented condition of oppression. The truly oppressed—Jews under the Nazis, Tutsis under the Hutus, the Armenians under the Turks, Syrians under Assad, Libyans under Gadafi, Chileans under Pincochet, Mexicans under the drug cartels, Chinese victims of the Cultural Revolution, blacks, Hispanics, Asians, and native Americans under American apartheid, sexual minorities in many societies, women going back millennia in numerous cultures, and so on—seem to constitute one of history's unbroken traditions.

The arrogation of the appalling conditions of tyranny, torture, execution, disappearance, and victimization to contemporary American conditions profoundly distorts reality in service to psychological distress and a self-aggrandizing narcissism of social welfare practice. Neither authenticity nor culture is heritable. The suffering of ancestors is not a genetic event. Surely some Americans, perhaps even many, do not receive the resources or dignity they deserve, and criminal justice in the United States remains an oxymoron. Just as surely, American society, open and democratic as it is, does not oppress people, contrary to the seductions of "oppression, however minor" (Burghardt, 135). To apply oppression to the United States is to create an imaginary justification for revolutionary change and, perversely, an imaginary basis for an acquiescent practice. Professional certification that requires a fake baptism in the wounds of true victims gives up on pragmatic services that are accountable to concrete goals and becomes a bauble of its own romantic retreat from both history and service to those in need.

The following passage by Alain Finkelkraut is drawn from an anthology of commentaries by the children of Holocaust survivors:

> The cherubic, over-nourished, potbellied men fancy themselves to be Isrolik, little Tom Thumb of the ghetto, the waif of the streets. They mask their inborn softness with the outcast's courage. But the bravado is false. To these mama's boys, Jewish history is a lullaby, the song that peoples their sleep with heroic dreams and permits them vicarious experience of the horror. Cowards in life, martyred in dream—they love historical self-deception, confusing the sheltered world in which they live with the cataclysm [of the Holocaust that] their parents endured. Among Jews they constitute a strange widespread category, one that has not yet found a name. They are not religious, at least most of them; in vain they cherish Jewish culture, possessing only its sorry relics. They have not performed their apprenticeship to Judaism under the gaze of the Other. . . . They are unwavering Jews, but armchair Jews, since, after the Catastrophe, Judaism cannot offer them any content but suffering, and they themselves do not suffer. In order to deny this contradiction, they have chosen to pass their time in a novelistic space full of sound and fury that offers them the best role.... They have taken up residence in fiction. The Judaism they invoke enraptures and transports them magically to a setting in which they are exalted and sanctified. For these habitues of unreality, more numerous than one might suppose, I propose the name "imaginary Jews." (Finkelkraut, 367–68)

Just as there are "imaginary Jews" who confuse "the sheltered world in which they live with the cataclysm their parents endured," so too, there are imaginary Christians who never faced the lions but who declaim from the Cross and yearn for stigmata; imaginary blacks still insisting that they live in plantation slavery; imaginary Latinos— "pobrecitos" all—still deeply embittered by haciendados and patrones; imaginary Moslems in retreat from the modern world; imaginary Mormons thirsty and hungry on the trek from Nauvoo, Illinois to Utah; imaginary Southerners gaunt from the siege of Atlanta and pining for the lost Southern way of life; imaginary Native Americans still scarred from the Trail of Tears; imaginary feminists thwarted in their life's ambitions by their comfortable homes and indulgent fathers; and imaginary empowerment practitioners who invent the liberation and empowerment of the many imagined oppressed. But most pernicious of all is the imaginary suffering of the comfortable classes in America, endlessly complaining about their entitlement to ever greater comfort, income, and influence.

All of the imaginary oppressed suffer terribly from their fictive martyrdom. "Imaginary people, more numerous than one might suppose," have "taken up residence in fiction" (ibid., 368). The sentimentality they "invoke enraptures and transports them magically to a setting in which they are exalted and sanctified" (Finkelkraut, 368). Unfortunately, the setting is contemporary American social policy with its romantic attachment to ideologies of great socioeconomic inequality.

The imaginary oppressed precipitate and perhaps even collude in a real social welfare policy that propagates the illusion of service, the questionable virtues of American sentimentality and its presiding attachment to romantic social welfare values. Empowerment practice is as enraptured with the nation's extreme individualism and the ability of the individual to perform heroic deeds of liberation as the very ethos that it claims to disparage. Thus, psychotherapy and counseling play a core role in both liberation practice and mainstream practice, which seeks adaptation with no appreciation for the fact that neither has demonstrated a capacity to achieve their goals. The humor in the situation is stretched out to dryness by the seemingly permanent deprivations and isolation of perhaps half the nation.

Empowerment practice has gone through a sly conversion: liberation has become a personal responsibility. Thus, failure to free oneself of deprivation is a sign of character failure that justifies the deprivation. Notwithstanding the plangent commitment to the strengths perspective, the field typically describes the so-called "oppressed" as though they were the peasants, the serfs, "the normal primitives" of American society quivering with oppressed helplessness and piteous need for the liberationist ministrations of empowerment revolutionaries (Swigert and Farrell 1977). Yet, the passivity both of the poor and of the ethnic and gender targets of empowerment practice signals a freely chosen acceptance of the status quo. This uncoerced choice contradicts the liberationist's scenario of oppression. The so-called "oppressed," by and large, do not consider themselves in dire peril. There is very little to be said for efforts to improve the lot of impoverished and marginalized people that mischaracterizes their needs and that condescendingly attributes their social and political predicaments to misguided, uninformed, and willfully inaccurate assumptions about the world. In just this way, empowerment practice confirms the isolation of those in need from full membership in the society. Contemporary empowerment practice is not what the early insurrectionists had in mind.

Reactionary Tribalism and Empowerment Practice

The mass movements that improved life for poorer and marginalized groups in the United States (or were simply coincidental with improvements) are atrophied in sectarian empowerment practices. They are memorials to those movements in the manner of civil war battle reenactments, inscriptions on funerary urns, plastic busts of Beethoven, and statues of saints which affirm the values that contemporaries impose on them rather than their original meaning. Empowerment agencies are political spoils and employment programs for staff rather than assistance for those in need. Social work and the other helping professions, notably psychotherapy and counseling, are institutionalized remnants rather than continuations of the mass movements.

To carry the assumption of pernicious prejudice into the present perpetuates as convenient fiction what was once devastatingly real. It encourages a revanchist bigotry of sectarian liberation practice that cannot succeed in any regard but to create competition among people in need. The sanctimony and righteousness of the imagined oppressed divide people with common interests, dissipating political pressure for greater socioeconomic equality and facilitating the minimalism of contemporary American social welfare policy. The reactionary tribalism of the imaginary oppressed—a pathetic prejudice coming from those who most suffer from it—abetted by the romantic sentimentalities of the helping professions rigidify group boundaries with nostalgia for cultural preservation. Reactionary tribalism retards the acquiescence in a common culture of decency that, with fits and starts, tempts the United States.

The insistence on gender, ethnicity, race, and sex as primary identities simplifies American society as biological destiny—immutable social conditions in the steel of genetics. The logic behind a segregated practice of empowerment repeats the fallacy of immanence but this time for the convenience of the liberal imagination, such as it is. Moreover, the empowerment literature that nurtures contemporary practice has failed to identify the unique attributes of any supposedly oppressed group which distinguishes their members from the common culture or that justifies a segregated practice. Socioeconomic need—the class agenda—and subtle institutional forms of discrimination are common afflictions of almost all needy groups. However, at the hands of empowerment practice, groups of the needy are isolated behind vain fictions of unique suffering and, thus, unique claims for compensation.

The weakness of class-based movements in the United States is customarily attributed to the broad acceptance of heroic individualism and the rest of America's policy romanticism, often summed up as political conservatism. The most notable reform movements in the United States since WWII have pressed agendas for procedural reforms rather than substantive distributions of wealth or income. That is, the reform movements largely exerted pressure to extend the culture's basic rules and franchises rather than to institute more egalitarian policies that would entail the basic restructuring of American stratification. The civil rights movement, the women's movement, and the gay rights movement pressed for equal treatment but did not insist on compensatory programs for prior discrimination. The agenda of the consumers' movement highlighted the need for greater regulation and disclosure but rarely, if ever, questioned the basic distribution of access to consumerism. Quite notably, the poor people's campaigns of the 1960s largely failed, while the decline of labor unions since the 1950s parallels growing inequality. None of the successful movements challenged the basic tenets of the nation's policy romanticism but rather petitioned for greater access to the culture largely as it is. Indeed, the prevailing literature of gay rights, civil rights, and women's equality is fashioned off the dramatic narrative of heroic leadership and liberation.

In order to develop a constituency of the poor, the near poor, and low-paid vulnerable workers, people in these conditions must first acknowledge their common needs as well as their incapacity to succeed on their own. However, few citizens in these groups are willing to confess their own limitations and suffer isolation from the American fellowship of independence and success. In this sense, economic failure in the United States confers the stigma of social failure and, because it implies personal irresponsibility, moral failure as well. The American ethos expressed through policy romanticism treats personal failure as tantamount to sacrilege and treason that place the individual beyond civic redemption.

The insistence on the individual's capacity for heroic overcoming, that is, redemption through self-liberation, runs through empowerment practice and its devotion to Saleebey's strengths perspective, establishing itself as a sacramental church of the American faith. In its evocation of romantic policy that inhibits effective responses to social need, empowerment practice reinforces the reactionary tribalism of American society.

The soft bigotry of empowerment practice is predicated on a mindless nostalgia for cultural preservation as though each subculture and immigrant culture comprises a national treasure that contributes to diversity and strength. Cultural preservation imposes a rigidity on American class and caste lines that dissipates pressures for common institutions and a shared destiny. It clutters economic and civic progress with rebarbative ethnocentricities papered over as necessities of helping. It also ignores the reality that many immigrant groups bring along ferocious intolerances, authoritarian and caste-based attitudes, and deep hostility to democratic tenets of tolerance. Similarly, a substantial number of the intended beneficiaries of empowerment practice also perpetuate a dysfunctional chauvinism and other values that are antagonistic to the decencies of an open democracy. Thus, so-called "oppressed groups"—native and immigrant—embarking on the revolutionary path to empowerment, might first be liberated from the hatreds of their own tribal existences.

The contribution of empowerment practice to cultural preservation and to the nation's reactionary tribalism has the insidious effect of converting frank deprivation into the blessings of freely chosen membership in a protective subculture.[1] In this way, deprivations in education, jobs, income support, and the rest are maintained as prudent policy abstinence out of respect for the diversity of American society; that is, the unique anthropological cleverness of needy groups in developing creative solutions to social challenges. This convenient tolerance for deprivation as a cultural art form and a sacred tribal rite reduces pressure for redistributive national policies while endorsing program strategies such as empowerment practice that keep the deprived politically and socially separated from each other. Unfortunately, the liberationist mentality is slowly relegating the needy to natural history dioramas.

Even the merest suggestion of ethnic, racial, and gender specialness—that is often the defining element of empowerment practice and is presumably adopted with the best intentions—hints at natural superiority and natural entitlement. It recalls the prejudices associated with the greatest atrocities of human existence. The justifications for segregated practice in the developmental pretenses of social treatment are little different in form than eugenics, the divine rights of kings, ethnic cleansing, caste systems, Pope Innocent VIII's (a riotous misnomer) textbook for the inquisitions of the counterreformation (Kramer and Spenger 1971), and the rest of civilization's shop of horrors. The romantic vision—a horrid distortion of civilization—as political regime has been an awful tyranny.

Empowerment practice has passed into the proverbs of the helping professions. If it has any meaning, empowerment and empowerment practice are legitimized by the grievous conditions of oppression. Its goals are political even when its strategies may entail psychological tactics and direct service. However, the meaning of empowerment has been broadened and cheapened by its application to nearly any grievance, often measured simply as subjective discontent. In this way, improving human capacity has become equated to empowerment, in effect, supplanting the political pursuit of egalitarian justice and, thus, attention to the claims of poor and marginalized groups. The only political content left in empowerment practice is a stylish reference to extremism of belief but, of course, not action. Empowerment has come to mean little more than "enabling," which itself has little meaning. Empowerment practice is but one of the many ways that the helping professions enact obedience to democratic populism and its sectarian provincialism, as though old injustices could be rectified by symbolic triumphs and loyalty to romantic impossibilities.

The empowerment professional imposes a complex notion of the world and its failings on the helping situation. It is convenient for practice but hardly constitutes value-neutral, patient-centered practice. What is the value of good intentions, if indeed they prevail in the helping professions, if they are so oblivious of the outcomes of their actions and their social meaning?

Democratic Populism and Empowerment Practice vs. Democratic Progressivism

Richard Hoftadter (1963) put his finger on an important trait of American politics and society. However, anti-intellectualism is not marginal and recurrent but persistent and dominant in policy making. It is but one expression of American policy romanticism that emerges from the nation's preference for gnomic knowing, its deeply superstitious rejection of objectivity and coherence in favor of magical thinking, and a pervasive sense of the role of the divine in everyday life. The flamboyant instances of anti-intellectualism in American history—just to name a few, Joseph McCarthy and red-baiting, the Great Awakening of the eighteenth century, the second awakening of the nineteenth century, fundamentalist religion generally, the Know Nothings, and numerous other politically reactionary groups such as the John Birch Society and the Tea Party—are not the most telling instances of anti-intellectual and romantic social policy. Rather, the prevailing and continuous social policy of the United States, in particular its social welfare policies, embodies the tenets of policy romanticism. It enacts an exaggerated individualism and justifies itself in terms of self-evident truths and the certainties of belief predicated on faith in an imagined American tradition that confers an inevitable right to lead all nations.

America has become a hyperdemocracy with functionally universal adult enfranchisement. It is the most open society that has ever existed, exercising little coercion and even less oppression of its citizens. Its prevailing policies represent the consensus of its citizens. However, the consensus is formed less through a national narrative that approximates reasoned discourse but more through the small and large choices of citizens as they go about their lives. Their daily consumption of reality summates to institutionalized preferences through a competition of detached roles that are naturally aggregated in the nation's near infinity of formal and informal organizations. Each role choice that a citizen makes—purchases of goods, where to live, how to marry, how many children to have, what to eat and wear, who to associate with, and so on—gives informal strength to organizations that depend on those choices. In this way, vegetarians lend vegetable producers and their organizations political, social, and commercial strength relative to meat producers; and to the degree to which money and attention are captured by vegetable producers, their importance and their claims on public attention rise relative to all other organizations. The strength is given without ever joining a formal organization of vegetable producers. Each role organization competes not only in markets for profits but also in politics for public policy preference and socially for status.[2]

Thus, through the individual choices of American citizens and the sorting of role organizations, national priorities expressed as social institutions as well as public policy carry a profound social sanction. In this sense, public policy is the end product, the ratification, of an immensely open and continuing social process that adjudicates informally but no less powerfully among the multiplicity of citizen preferences. The process of detached roles accounts for the immense stability of the United States, which enjoys the oldest continuous government in the world today. Unfortunately, the preferences that animate the process—the deeply held priorities of the American people—are romantic more than they are pragmatic.

Policy romanticism is realized politically as democratic populism in the United States. Democratic progressivism with its core commitment to pragmatism in policy making is a minor political theme in American politics. The march of democratic progressivism in the United States to greater socioeconomic equality has stumbled on democratic populism, a construction of both American liberals and conservatives. The liberal's entente with American romanticism is also an accommodation with American conservatism and signals a rejection of progressive reform. Both liberals and conservatives accept the American approach to social policy: inexpensive and culturally compatible social services that customarily emphasize individual responsibility over social responsibility in the meanness of their provisions as well as in their ceremonial affirmation of American romanticism. In just this way, contemporary empowerment practice and its soft bigotries are inventions of democratic populism. They conjure a fake process of liberation segregated into factions and addressing individual deficits but without a political or social strategy of change. At least the early radicals focused their communal fantasies on political activism, subsuming individual liberation within the dynamics of communal insurrection. Instead, empowerment practice conforms to the policy romanticism of individual responsibility. The association of empowerment practice and liberation with the New Left is a synergy of hypocrisy.

Even so, the most disturbing impetus of romantic policy making is the contrivance of an underclass, a group of people who are usually poor; scorned, stigmatized, and isolated from American culture; and, as imagined threats to American progress, serve as one of democratic populism's convenient scapegoats (Gans 1995). This has indeed been the vector of American social welfare policy. Since 1973, the benefits of cash welfare had been steadily eroded by the time Aid to Families of Dependent Children (AFDC) was replaced in 1996 by Temporary Assistance to Needy Families (TANF). The change eliminated welfare as a right, reduced eligibility in most cases to sixty months of benefits, capped the federal contribution, vastly increased state control and the discretion of welfare agencies over the lives of recipients, and continued to reduce benefits. The reauthorization of TANF in 2006 further reduced benefits and intensified the antagonism of the legislation to the poor. The characterization of the poor as malingerers and misfits that pervaded AFDC became manifest in even the title of the new legislation: The Personal Responsibility and Work Opportunity Act of 1996 (PRWOA). The PRWOA also cut back on federal contributions to nutrition and food programs, notably Food Stamps, while also eliminating the eligibility of immigrants, addicts, and many poor children for a variety of benefits.

The legislation continues to be immensely popular. Personal responsibility exemplified through work has been the touchstone of American relief and its blind insistence that work was always available to those willing to work. However, the softer edges of the earlier legislation were sharpened by the increasing movement of the populist consensus to the right, that is, toward a greater embrace of policy romanticism. Slowly, the romantic imagination in the United States is coming to criminalize poverty and failure as felonies of the spirit.

The refusal to correct the initial economic distributions of the market and complacency with American stratification are codified in the nation's dominant social welfare programs as well as in its cash welfare programs. There is little sharing in Social Security (Old Age, Survivors, and Disability Insurance) whose benefits are largely proportionate to contributions and quite inadequate for the most needy; even after a lifetime of work, there is little forgiveness for working at low wages. In fact, in 2004, more than half of single-aged Social Security beneficiaries lived on less than $15,000 per year, while about 30 percent of aged beneficiary couples lived on less than $25,000 per year (Epstein 2010). Moreover, the most deserving Americans—poor children without parents and the poor who are totally and permanently disabled—are provided benefits through child welfare and the Supplemental Security Income programs that are below the very low American poverty level, even when including food and housing assistance (US Congress House 2008).

In contrast with democratic populism, democratic progressivism has been a persistent but minor theme in the United States. It pursues a meritrocratic society, that is, democratically sanctioned governance by the most capable and qualified. However, it rejects the notion that unregulated or loosely regulated markets will create a fair meritocracy. Thus, democratic progressivism accepts responsibility for assuring the nation's social welfare through public interventions into both society and markets. Democratic progressivism entails the pragmatic evaluation of its interventions. It discards unsuccessful social welfare programs along with imaginary goals.

The core progressive tenet which inspires its interventions holds that social influences rather than individual character best explain people's behaviors and social outcomes. Stated differently, people are not their own invention but largely a summation of concrete factors that impinge on their development. In the face of social problems, solutions intervene with those tangible factors. This enormously offends the American consensus of policy romanticism and democratic populism to deny the soul except as a literary device and to speak only of the concrete: resources, employment, education, the family, the community, and so forth. However, pragmatism requires the Enlightenment's hope of a functional science of humanity that unfortunately still eludes the social sciences.

The conciliation with social imperatives is unavoidable for a social welfare agency, although empowerment practice seems to have replaced reluctant adaptation with smug convenience. The liberation of the oppressed is estimable and humane, but the perpetuation of dead memorials to this goal—an empty practice and a disingenuous literature—is a waste of reformist energy. The worst that can be said about empowerment practice is that it buttresses the ethnocentricity of American society despite its pot-banging for liberation and the inability to achieve any goal. Its mean-spirited hypocrisy falls short of tragic paradox but still pays tribute to the pervasive influence of democratic populism and its demands for obedient ceremony. It is good that empowerment practice and the helping professions fail as liberators, especially as their notion of where to go and what to be liberated from is as malleable and amenable to tyranny as the theological imagination that found grounds for American slavery in the Bible and protected the innocent souls of citizens with the auto-da-fe.

Notes

1. Michaels (2006) discusses the trade-off between cultural preservation as diversity on the one hand and equality on the other.
2. The ecology of detached roles is detailed in Epstein (2010). There is also much that suggests a detached role theory in Canetti's (1963) *Masse und Macht*, translated as *Crowds and Power*, as well as the literature on mass movements. Canetti attempts to detail the social influence of unreasoned popular preferences. This observation has often been ignored in considerations of policy making in the United States that seem trapped in tributes to the rationality of its democracy—its chosenness as the apotheosis of the Enlightenment in promise, if not in fact—even when quite critical of its

imperfections. However, *masse* also translates as mob, and certainly much of the book deals with the passion of mobs and not simply large aggregations of people, that is, crowds. Still, "crowd" better conveys than "mob" a relatively permanent momentum, an irresistible force of the popular will that may be quite unreasoned. Democratic populism adopts the sense of long-standing crowd preferences that have been institutionalized in society and enacted in its laws. It can be as unreasoned and as vengeful as mob behavior and spawn a variety of devoted cults. Indeed, the interventions of empowerment practice (and of the helping professions generally) contain much of this sort of impassioned, gnomic certitude and while dressed up as professional wisdom, they proceed largely as a stolid, intractable herd led by culture.

Acknowledgments

I am grateful to the following people for assistance with the manuscript: Harris Chaiklin, Robert Dippner, Paul Epstein, Ronald A. Farrell, Joel Fischer, Jorge and Carolyn Grossman, Amris Henry, Gary Holden, Walter Benn Michaels, Brij Mohan, Paul Moloney, Masha Pisarenko, David Smail, David Stoesz, Noriko Takeda, Joanne Thompson, and Saundra Weatherup. A special note of thanks to a very special research assistant, Salina Bahk, and also gratitude for David Stoesz's documentation of the academic depravity of social work in *A Dream Deferred* that provided the context for the present work. Errors that remain after their good counsel are surely the result of hidden conspiracies, malicious spirits, and the reader's misperceptions.

The book could not have been written without the complicity between the growing tribalism in American society and the long-standing hypocrisies of the helping professions, notably social work, as well as counseling, psychotherapy, the suite of management enthusiasms, public health, health promotion, and the like. Rather than press for greater socioeconomic equality and confront the ineffectiveness of their minimal interventions, the helping professions have grown complacent with the "bribes to indolence" of status appointments and lower standards. The decline of quality is most noticeable in the academy. Without the incompetence and ethnocentricity of the helping professions, acquiescent university administrations, and the growing depravity of America's civic culture, this book would have been impossible. My gratitude to all those who kneel at social convenience is only lessened by my sadness that it is so.

Universal values and a civic culture of decency seem lost in the retreat to fantasies of tribal virtue, ignoring the wisdom of ages that the weak are only protected within the arms of a culture that accepts all minorities, not just theirs, and extends rights to all citizens, not just compensation to a select few who happen to be the repositories of ephemeral pity. Many beneficiaries of the painful struggle for a decent common culture sit complacently in positions they have not earned and do not honor by continuing effort. They and their disciplines are the thankless children of America's progressive tradition. There is humor in tragedy as each and both together fulfill themselves through the clowns who act out the street theater of empowerment practice.

References

Allen-Meares, P., and C. Garvin. 2000. *The Handbook of Social Work Direct Practice*. Thousand Oaks, CA: Sage Publications.

Andrews, A. B., P. S. Motes, A. G. Floyd, V. C. Flerx, and A. Lopez-De Fede. 2005. "Building Evaluation Capacity in Community-based Organizations: Reflections of an Empowerment Evaluation Team." *Journal of Community Practice* 13, no. 4: 85–104

Angelides, P., B. Thomas, B. Born, D. Holtz-Eakin, B. Georgiou, H. Murren, B. Graham, J. W. Thompson, K. Hennessey, and P. J. Wallison. 2011. *The Financial Crisis Inquiry Report*. http://fcic.law.stanford.edu/report (last accessed date 12/15/11).

Angelique, H. L., T. M. Reischl, and W. S. Davidson II. 2002. "Promoting Political Empowerment: Evaluation of an Intervention with University Students." *American Journal of Community Psychology* 30, no. 6: 815–33

Angell, M. 2011a. "The Epidemic of Mental Illness." *New York Review of Books*, June 23.

———. 2011b. "The Illusions of Psychiatry." *New York Review of Books*, July 14.

———. 2011c. "The Illusions of Psychiatry: An Exchange Reply." *New York Review of Books* 58, no. 13.

Baeck, L. 1970. *Judaism and Christianity*. New York: Scribner.

Baillie, L., S. Broughton, J. Bassett-Smith, W. Aasen, M. Oostindie, B. A. Marino, and K. Hewitt. 2004. "Community Health, Community Involvement, and Community Empowerment: Too Much to Expect?" *Journal of Community Psychology* 32, no. 2: 217–28.

Ball, B., P. K. Kerig, and B. Rosenbluth. 2009. "Like a Family but Better because You can Actually Trust Each Other: The Expect Respect Dating Violence Prevention Program for at-risk Youth." *Health Promotion Practice* 10, no. 1: 45S–58S.

Barreto, M. A. 2007. "Si Se Puede!-Latino Candidates and the Mobilization of Latino Voters." *American Political Science Review* 101, no. 3: 425–41.

Beck, B. 1983. *Empowerment: A Future Goal of Social Work*. New York: CSS Working Papers in Social Policy.

Beck, J. S. 1995. *Cognitive Therapy: Basics and Beyond*. New York: Guilford Press.

Bellamy, C. D., and C. T. Mowbray. 1998. "Supported Education as an Empowerment Intervention for People with Mental Illness." *Journal of Community Psychology* 26, no. 5: 401–13.

Bentley, S. 1978. "Book Reviews: The Declining Significance of Race: Blacks and Changing American Institutions by W.J. Wilson." *Race Class* 20: 200–201.

Berg, M., E. Coman, and J. J. Schensul. 2009. "Youth Action Research for Prevention: A Multi-level Intervention Designed to Increase Efficacy and Empowerment among Urban Youth." *American Journal of Community Psychology* 43, no. 3–4: 345–59.

Berkeley, K. C. 1999. *The Women's Liberation Movement in America*. Westport, CT: Greenwood Press.

Berkowitz, B. 2001. "Studying the Outcomes of Community-based Coalitions." *American Journal of Community Psychology* 29, no. 2: 213–27.

Biegel, D., and A. Naperste. 1982. "The Neighborhood and Family Services Project: An Empowerment Model Linking Clergy, Agency, Professionals and Community Residents." In *Community Mental Health and Behavioral Ecology*, ed. A. Jeger and R. Slotnick, 303–18. New York: Plenum.

Bock, S. 1980. "Conscientization: Paolo Friere and Class-based Practice." *Catalyst* 2: 5–25.

Boehm, A., and L. H. Staples. 2002. "The Functions of the Social Worker in Empowering: The Voices of Consumers and Professionals." *Social Work* 47, no. 4: 449–60.

———. 2004. "Empowerment: The Point of View of Consumers." *Families in Society: The Journal of Contemporary Social Services* 85, no. 2: 270–80.

Boydell, K. M., and T. Volpe. 2004. "A Qualitative Examination of the Implementation of a Community-Academic Coalition." *Journal of Community Psychology* 32, no. 4: 359–74.

Brenner, J. 2000. *Women and the Politics of Class*. New York: Monthly Review Press.

Bukiet, M. J., ed. 2002. *Nothing Makes You Free: Writings by Descendants of Jewish Holocaust Survivors*. 1st ed. New York: W.W. Norton.

Burckhardt, C. S., S. R. Clark, C. A. OReilly, and R. M. Bennett. 1997. "Pain-coping Strategies of Women with Fibromyalgia: Relationship to Pain, Fatigue, and Quality of Life." *Journal of Musculoskeletal Pain* 5, no. 3, 37–49.

Burghardt, S. 1982. *The Other Side of Organizing*. Cambridge, MA: Schenkman.

Burt, M. R., and D. S. Nightingale. 2010. *Repairing the US Social Safety Net*. Washington, DC: Urban Institute Press.

Burtless, G. 2007. "What Have We Learned about Poverty and Inequality? Evidence from Cross-national Analysis." *Focus* 25, no. 1: 12–17.

Bush, D. M. 1992. "Womens Movements and State Policy Reform Aimed at Domestic Violence against Women – A Comparison of the Consequences of Movement Movilization in the United States and India." *Gender & Society* 6, no. 4: 587–608.

Canetti, E. 1963. *Crowds and Power*. New York: The Viking Press.

Carr, E. S. 2003. "Rethinking Empowerment Theory Using a Feminist Lens: The Importance of Process." *AFFILIA* 18, no. 1: 8–20.

Carballo-Dieguez, A., C. Dolezal, C. S. Leu, L. Nieves, F. Diaz, C. Decena, and I. Balan. 2005. "A Randomized Controlled Trial to Test an HIV-prevention Intervention for Latino Gay and Bisexual Men: Lessons Learned." *AIDS Care-Psychological and Socio-Medical Aspects of AIDS/HIV* 17, no. 3: 314–28.

Carkhuff, R. R., and C. B. Truax. 1965. "Training in Counseling and Psychotherapy: An Evaluation of an Integrated Didactic and Experimental Approach." *Journal of Consulting Psychology* 29, no. 4: 333–36.

Chadiha, L. A., P. Adams, D. E. Biegel, W. Auslander, and L. Gutierrez. 2004. "Empowering African American Women Informal Caregivers: A Literature Synthesis and Practice Strategies." *Social Work* 49, no. 1.

Chaiklin, H. 2011. "Attitudes, Behavior and Social Practice." *Journal of Sociology and Social Welfare* 38, no. 1: 31–54.

Chan, C. L., Y. Chan, and V. W. Lou. 2002. "Evaluating an empowerment group for divorced Chinese women in Hong Kong." *Research on Social Work Practice* 12, no. 4: 558–69.

Checkoway, B., and A. Norsman. 1986. "Empowering Citizens with Disabilities." *Community Development Journal* 21: 270–77.

Chronister, K. M., and E. H. McWhirter. 2003. "Applying Social Cognitive Career Theory to the Empowerment of Battered Women." *Journal of Counseling & Development* 81, no. 4: 418–25.

Cohen, M. 1988. *The Sisterhood: The True Story of the Women who Changed the World.* New York: Simon and Schuster.

Combs, G. and J. Freedman. 1990. *Symbol, Story, and Ceremony: Using Metaphor in Individual and Family Therapy.* New York: Norton.

Coontz, S. 1992. *The Way We Never Were.* New York: Basic Books.

———. 2011. *A Strange Stirring: The Feminine Mystique and American Women at the Dawn of the 1960's.* New York: Basic Books.

Coontz, S., and P. Henderson. 1986. *Women's Work Men's Property.* London: Verso.

Coppola, M., and R. Rivas. 1985. "The Task-action Group Technique: A Case Study of Empowering Elderly." In *Innovations in Social Group Work: Feedback from Practice to Theory,* ed. M. Parenes, 133–47. New York: Haworth.

Coser, L. 1956. *The Functions of Social Conflict.* Glencoe, IL: Free Press.

Cox, C. B. 2002. "Empowering African American Custodial Grandparents." *Social Work* 47, no. 1: 45–54.

Davis, A. Y. 1988. "Radial Perspectives on the Empowerment of Afro-American Women: Lessons for the 1980's." *Harvard Education Review* 58, no. 3: 348–53.

Dhaene, M. T. 1995. "Evaluation of Feminist-based Adolescent Group Therapy." *Smith College Studies in Social Work* 65, no. 2: 153–66.

DeNavas-Walt, C., B. D. Proctor, and C. Lee. 2006. "U.S. Census Bureau, Current Population Reports, P60-231." *Income, Poverty, and Health Insurance Coverage in the United States: 2005.* Washington, DC: U.S. Government Printing Office.

DeNavas-Walt, C., B. D. Proctor, and J. Smith. 2007. "U.S. Census Bureau, Current Population Reports, P60-233." *Income, Poverty, and Health Insurance Coverage in the United States: 2006.* Washington, DC: U.S. Government Printing Office.

———. 2008. "U.S. Census Bureau, Current Population Reports, P60-235." *Income, Poverty, and Health Insurance Coverage in the United States: 2007.* Washington, DC: U.S. Government Printing Office.

———. 2009. "U.S. Census Bureau, Current Population Reports, P60-236." *Income, Poverty, and Health Insurance Coverage in the United States: 2008.* Washington, DC: U.S. Government Printing Office.

———. 2010. "U.S. Census Bureau, Current Population Reports, P60-238." *Income, Poverty, and Health Insurance Coverage in the United States: 2009.* Washington, DC: U.S. Government Printing Office.

———.2011. "U.S. Census Bureau, Current Population Reports, P60-239." *Income, Poverty, and Health Insurance Coverage in the United States: 2010.* Washington, DC: U.S. Government Printing Office.

Denby, R. R., and S. Owens-Kane, S. 2004. "African American Families, Mental Health, and Living Cooperatives: A Program and Research Analysis." In *Reconceptualizing the Strengths and Common Heritage of Black Families: Practice, Research, and Policy Issues.* Springfield, IL: Charles C. Thomas.

Dillard, A. D. 2001. *Guess Who's Coming to Dinner Now? Multicultural Conservatism in America.* New York: New York University Press.

Dineen, T. 1996. *Manufacturing Victims.* Montreal: Robert Davies Publishing.

Diversi, M., and C. Mecham. 2005. "Latino(a) Students and Caucasian Mentors in a Rural After-school Program: Towards Empowering Adult-youth Relationships." *Journal of Community Psychology* 33, no. 1: 31–40.

Dodenhoff, D. 1998. "Is Welfare Really about Social Control?" *Social Service Review* (September): 310–36.

Domina, L. 2004. *Understanding Ceremony.* Westport, CT: Greenwood Press.

Dunlap, K. M. 1997. "Family empowerment: one outcome of cooperative preschool education." *Child Welfare* 76, no. 4: 501–18.

Echols, A. 1989. *Daring to be Bad: Radical Feminism in America 1967-1975.* Minneapolis: University of Minnesota Press.

Edwards, H. 1979. "Review: The Declining Significance of Race: Blacks and Changing American Institutions." *Social Forces* 57, no. 3: 990–93.

Eisner, D. A. 2000. *The Death of Psychotherapy.* Westport, CT: Praeger.

Epstein, W. M. 1995. *The Illusion of Psychotherapy.* New Brunswick, NJ: Transaction Publishers.

———. 2004. Cleavage in American Attitudes toward Social Welfare. *Journal of Sociology and Social Welfare* 31, no. 4: 175–99.

———. 2006. *Psychotherapy as Religion: The Civil Divine in America.* Reno, NV: University of Nevada Press.

———. 2010. *Democracy without Decency: Good Citizenship and the War on Poverty.* State Park, PA: Penn State University Press.

———. 2011. *The Dilemma of American Social Welfare.* New Brunswick, NJ: Transaction Publishers.

Fagan, H. 1979. *Empowerment: Skills for Parish Social Action.* New York: Paulist Press.

Faludi, S. 1991. *Backlash: The Undeclared War against American Women.* New York: Crown.

Fanon, F. 1952. *Black Skin, White Masks.* New York: Grove Press.

———. 1963. *The Wretched of the Earth.* New York: Grove Press.

———. 1964. *Toward the African Revolution.* New York: Grove Press.

———. 1965. *A Dying Colonialism.* New York: Grove Weidenfeld.

Fay, B. 1987. *Critical Social Science.* Ithaca, NY: Cornell University Press.

Fetterman, D. M., S. J. Kaftarian, and A. Wanderson. 1996. *Empowerment Evaluation: Knowledge and Tools for Self-assessment and Accountability.* Thousand oaks, CA: Sage Publications.

Finkelkraut, A. 2002"The Protagonist Introduced." In *Nothing Makes You Free,* ed. L. J. Bukiet. New York: W.W. Norton.

Foster-Fishman, P. G., D. A. Salem, S. Chibnall, R. Legler, and C. Yapchai. 1998. "Empirical Support for the Critical Assumptions of Empowerment Theory." *American Journal of Community Psychology* 26, no. 4: 504–36.

Frain, M. P., and M. Bishop. 2009. "Empowerment Variables as Predictors of Outcomes in Rehabilitation." *Journal of Rehabilitation* 75, no. 1: 27–35.

Frank, J. D. 1973. *Persuasion and Healing—A Comparative Study of Psychotherapy.* Baltimore, MD: Johns Hopkins University Press.

Freire, P. 1970. *Pedagogy of the Oppressed.* New York: Penguin Books.

———. 1973. *Education for Critical Consciousness.* New York: The Seabury Press.

Friedan, B. 1963. *The Feminine Mystique.* New York: W.W. Norton.

Gans, H. 1995. *The War against the Poor: The Underclass and Antipoverty Policy.* New York: Basic Books.

Garcia-Reid, P., and R. J. Reid. 2009. "Finding Our Voices: Empowering Latino Students through Partnerships with School Social Workers." *School Social Work Journal* 33, no. 2: 57–69.

Garfinkel, H. 1956. "Conditions of Successful Degradation Ceremonies." *American Journal of Sociology* 61, no. 5: 420–24.

Garvin, C. "Work with Disadvantaged and Oppressed Groups." In *Individual Change through Small Groups*, ed. M. Sundel, P. Glasser, R. Sarri, and R. Vinter, 2nd ed., 461–72. New York: The Free Press, 1985.

Giardina, C. 2010. *Freedom for Women: Forging the Womens Liberation Movement, 1953-1970.* Gainesville: University Press of Florida.

Gibbs, D. A., S. R. Hawkins, A. M. Clinton-Sherrod, and R. K. Noonan. 2009. "Empowering Programs with Evaluation Technical Assistance: Outcomes and Lessons Learned." *Health Promotion Practice* 10, no. 1: 38S–44S.

Gist, M. E. 1987. "Self-efficacy: Implications for Organizational Behavior and Human Resource Management." *The Academy of Management Review* 12, no. 3: 472–85.

Gittell, R. J., and A. Vidal. 1998. *Community Organizing: Building Social Capital as a Development Strategy.* Thousand Oaks, CA: Sage Publications.

Gitterman, A., and C. B. Germain. 2008. *The Life Model of Social Work Practice.* New York: Columbia University Press.

Goffman, E. 1962. *Asylums: Essays on the Social Situation of Mental Patients and Other Inmates.* Chicago, IL: Aldine.

Gollub, E. L., K. M. Morrow, K. H. Mayer, B. A. Koblin, P. Brown Peterside, M. J. Husnik, and D. S. Metzger. 2010. "Three-city Feasibility Study of a Body Empowerment and HIV Prevention Intervention among Women with Drug Use Histories: Women FIT." *Journal of Women's Health* 19, no. 9: 1705–13.

Gordon-Bradhsaw, R. 1987. "A Social Essay on Special Issues Facing Poor Women of Color." *Women and Health* 12: 243–59.

Gould, K. 1987a. "Feminist Principles and Minority Concerns: Contributions, Problems, and Solutions." *Affilia: Journal of Women and Social Work* 3: 6–19.

———. 1987b. "Life Model vs. Conflict Model: A Feminist Perspective." *Social Work* 32: 346–51.

Graham, M. 2002. "Creating Spaces: Exploring the Role of Cultural Knowledge as a Source of Empowerment in Models of Social Welfare in Black Communities." *British Journal of Social Work* 32: 35–49.

Gross, M. L. 1978. *The Psychological Society.* New York: Random House.

Gusfield, J. R. 1963. *Symbolic Crusade: Status Politics and the American Temperance Movement.* Urbana, IL: University of Illinois Press.

Gusfield, J. R., and J. Michalowicz. 1984. "Secular Symbolism: Studies of Ritual, Ceremony, and Symbolic Order in Modern Life." *Annual Review Sociology* 10: 417–35.

Gutierrez, L. M. 1990. "Working with Women of Color: An Empowerment Perspective." *Social Work* 35, no. 2: 149–53.

Gutierrez, L. M., and R. Ortega. 1991. "Developing Methods to Empower Latinos: The Importance of Groups." *Social Work with Groups* 14, no. 2: 23–43.

Hamowy, R. 1987. *The Scottish Enlightenment and the Theory of Spontaneous Order.* Carbondale, IL: The University of Southern Illinois Press.

Hasenfield, Y. 1987. "Power in Social Work Practice." *Social Service Review* 61: 469–83.

Hawkins, S. R., A. M. Clinton-Sherrod, I. Neil, L. Hart, and S. J. Russel. 2009. "Logic Models as a Tool for Sexual Violence Prevention Program Development." *Health Promotion Practice* 10, no. 1: 29S–37S.

Hirayama, H., and K. Hirayama. 1985. "Empowerment through Group Participation: Process and Goal." In *Innovations in Social Group Work: Feedback from Practice to Theory*, ed. M. Parenes, 119–31. New York: Haworth.

Hofstadter, R. 1963. *Anti-Intellectualism in American Life.* New York: Vintage.

Horowitz, I. L. 1993. *The Decomposition of Sociology.* New York: Oxford University Press.

Horowitz, I. L., and J. Suchlicki. 2003. *Cuban Communisim 1959-2003.* New Brunswick, NJ: Transaction Publishers.

Howard, D. 1986. *The Dynamics of Feminist Therapy.* New York: The Haworth Press, 1986.

Hur, M. H. 2006. "Empowerment in Terms of Theoretical Perspectives: Exploring a Typology of the Process and Components across Disciplines." *Journal of Community Psychology* 34, no. 5: 523–40.

Ibanez, G. E., N. Khatchikian, C. A. Buck, D. L. Weisshaar, T. Abush-Kirsh, E. A. Lavizzo, and F. H. Norris. 2003. "Qualitative Analysis of Social Support and Conflict among Mexican and Mexican-American Disaster Survivors." *Journal of Community Psychology* 31, no. 1: 1–23.

Islam, G., and M. J. Zyphur. 2009. "Rituals of Organizations: A Review and Expansion on Current Theory." *Group & Organization Management* 34, no. 1: 114–39.

Itzhaky, H., and A. S. York. 2000. "Sociopolitical Control and Empowerment: An Extended Replication." *Journal of Community Psychology* 28, no. 4: 407–15.

Janoff-Bulman, R. 1979. "Characterological versus Behavior Self-blame: Inquiries into Depression and Rape." *Journal of Personality and Social Psychology* 37: 1798–810.

Jantii, M., et al. 2006. "American Exceptionalism in a New Light: A Comparison of Intergenerational Earnings Mobility in the Nordic Countries, the United Kingdom, and the United States." IZA Discussion Paper No. 1938. Bonn, Germany: IZA.

Jennings, J. 1979. "Review: The Declining Significance of Race in America by William Julius Wilson." *Review of Black Political Economy* 9, no. 4: 452–59.

Johnson, L. C. 1995. *Social Work Practice.* Boston, MA: Allyn and Bacon.

Jordan, J. V., A. G. Kaplan, J. B. Miller, I. P. Stivers, and J. L. Surrey.1991. *Women's Growth in Connection*. New York: The Guilford Press.

Kahneman, D. 2011. *Thinking, Fast and Slow*. New York: Farrar, Straus and Giroux.

Kaslow, N. J., A. S. Leiner, S. Reviere, E. Jackson, K. Bethea, J. Bhaju, M. Rhodes, M. Gantt, H. Senter, and M. P. Thompson. 2010. "Suicidal, Abused African American Women's Response to a Culturally Informed Intervention." *Journal of Consulting and Clinical Psychology* 78, no. 4: 449–58.

Keefe, T. 1976. "Empathy: The Critical Skill. *Social Work* 21, no. 1: 10–14.

———. 1980. "Empathy Skill and Critical Consciousness." *Social Casework* 61, no. 7: 387–93.

Kieffer, C. 1984. "Citizen Empowerment: A Developmental Perspective." In *Studies in Empowerment: Toward Understanding and Action*, ed. J. Rappaport, C. Swift, and R. Hess, 9–36). New York: Haworth.

Kirst-Ashman, K. K., and G. H. Hull, Jr. 2012. *Understanding Generalist Practice*. Belmont, CA: Brooks/Cole.

Koberg, C. S., W. Boss, J. C. Senjem, and E. A. Goodman. 1999. "Antecedents and outcomes of empowerment: Empirical evidence from the health care industry." *Group and Organization Management* 34, no. 1: 71–91.

Kopasci, R., and A. Faulkner. 1988. "The Powers that might be: The Unity of White and black feminists. *Affilia: Journal of Women and Social Work* 3: 33–50.

Kovach, A. C., J. Becker, and H. Worley. 2004. "The Impact of Community Health Workers on the Self-determination, Self-sufficiency, and Decision-making Ability of Low-Income Women and Mothers of Young Children. *Journal of Community Psychology* 32, no. 3: 343–56.

Kramer, H., J. Sprenger, and M. Summers. 1971. *The Malleus Maleficarum*. New York: Dover Publications.

Lafave, L., L. Desportes, and C. Mcbride. 2009. "Treatment Outcomes and Perceived Benefits: A Qualitative and Quantitative Assessment of a Women's Substance Abuse Treatment Program." *Women & Therapy* 32: 51–68.

Lapiere, R. T. 1965. *Social Change*. New York: McGraw Hill.

Laqueur, Walter. 2002. *Guerilla Warfare: A Historical and Critical Study*. New Brunswick, NJ: Transaction.

Larsen, M., C. C. Oldeide, and K. Malterud. 1997. "Not So Bad After All . . . Women's Experiences of Pelvic Examinations." *Family Practice* 14, no. 2: 148–52.

Larson, R., K. Walker, and N. Pearce. 2005. "A Comparison of Youth-driven and Adult-driven Youth Programs: Balancing Inputs from Youth and Adults." *Journal of Community Psychology* 33, no. 1: 57–74.

Leashore, B. R., H. L. McMurray, and B. C. Bailey. 1991. *Reuniting and Preserving African American Families* in Everett, J. E., S. S. Chipungu, and B. R. Leashore, *Child Welfare: An Afrocentric Approach*. New Brunswick, NJ: Rutgers University Press.

Lecroy, C. W. 2004. "The development and evaluation of an empowerment program for early adolescent girls." *Adolescence* 39: 427–41.

Lee, J.A.B. (1991). *The Empowerment Approach to Social Work Practice: Building the Beloved Community*. New York: Columbia University Press.

Leung, C., S. Tsang, and S. Dean. 2011. "Outcome Evaluation of the Hands-on Parent Empowerment (HOPE) Program." *Research on Social Work Practice* 2, no. 5: 549–61.

Lin-fu, J. 1987. "Special Health Concerns of Ethnic Minority Women." *Public Health Reports* 102: 12–14.

Longres, J., and E. Mcleod. 1980. "Consciousness Raising and Social Work Practice." *Social Casework* 61: 267–76.

Lopez, N. 2008. "Antiracist Pedagogy and Empowerment in a Bilingual Classroom in the US, circa 2006." *Theory into Practice* 47, no. 1: 43–50.

Maciak, B. J., R. Guzman, A. Santiago, G. Villalobos, and B. A. Isreal. 1999. "Establishing LA VIDA: A Community-based Partnership to Prevent Intimate Violence against Latina Women." *Health Education & Behavior* 26, no. 6: 821–40.

Man, D. 1999. "Community-based empowerment programme for families with a brain injured survivor: an outcome study." *Brain Injury* 13, no. 6: 433–45.

Manning, M. C., L. J. Cornelius, and J. N. Okundaye. 2004. "Empowering African Americans through Social Work Practice: Integrating an Afrocentric Perspective, Ego Psychology, and Spirituality." *Families in Society: The Journal of Contemporary Social Services* 85, no. 2.

Markward, M., and B. Yegidis. 2011. *Evidence-based Practice with Women: Toward Effective Social Work Practice with Low-income Women.* Los Angeles, CA: Sage Publications.

Martinez-Brawley, E. E., and P. Zorita. 2006. "Language, Identity, and Empowerment: The Case of Spanish in the Southwest." *Journal of Ethical & Cultural Diversity in Social Work* 15, no. 1/2: 81–95.

Mathieu, J. E., L. L. Gilson, and T. M. Ruddy. 2006. "Empowerment and team effectiveness: an empirical test of an integrated model." *Journal of Applied Psychology* 91, no. 1: 97–108.

Mathis, T., and D. Richan. 1986, March. *Empowerment: Practice in Search of Theory.* Paper presented at the Annual Program Meeting of the Council on Social Work Education, Miami, FL.

Maxwell, S. 2009. *Success and Solitude: Feminist Organizations Fifty Years after The Feminine Mystique.* Lanham, MD: University Press of America.

Mazumder, B. 2005. "Fortunate Sons: New Estimated of Intergenerational Mobility in the United States Using Social Security Earnings Data." *Review of Economics and Statistics* 87, no. 2: 235–55.

McFarlane, J., and J. Fehir. 1994. "De madres a madres: A Community, Primary Health Care Program Based on Empowerment." *Health Education Quarterly* 21, no. 3: 381–94.

McGoldrick, M., J. Giordano, and N. Garcia-Preto. 2005. *Ethnicity and Family Therapy.* New York: Guilford Press.

Mein, S. 1998 "Concerns and Misconceptions about Cardiovascular Disease Risk Factors: A Focus Group Evaluation with Low-income Hispanic Women." *Hispanic Journal of Behavioral Sciences* 20, no. 2: 192–211.

Meyer, J. W. and B. Rowan. 1977. "Institutional Organizations: Formal Structure as Myth and Ceremony." *American Journal of Sociology* 83: 340–63.

Michaels, W. B. 2006. *The Trouble with Diversity Eloquently: How We Learn to Love Diversity and Hate Equality.* New York: Metropolitan Books.

Miller, R. L., and R. Campbell. 2006. "Taking Stock in Empowerment Evaluation: An Empirical Review." *American Journal of Evaluation* 27, no. 3: 296–319.

Mishra, S. I., L. R. Chavez, J. R. Magana, P. Nava, R. B. Valdez, and F. A. Hubbel. 1998. "Improving Breast Cancer Control among Latinas: Evaluation of a Theory-based Educational Program." *Health Education & Behavior* 25, no. 5: 653–70.

References

Moloney, P. Forthcoming. *The Psychology Industry.* London: Pluto Press.

Moody, K. A., J. C. Childs, and S. B. Sepples. 2003. "Intervening with at risk youth: evaluation of the youth empowerment and support program." *Pediatric Nursing* 29, no. 4: 263–70.

Moreau, M. J. 1990. "Empowerment through Advocacy and Consciousness Raising: Implications of a Structural Approach to Social Work." *Journal of Sociology and Social Welfare,* no. 1 2: 53–67.

Morell, C. 1987. "Cause is Function: Toward a Feminist Model of Integration for Social Work." *Social Service Review* 61: 144–55.

Morris, Al. 1996. "What's Race Got to Do with It?" *Contemporary Sociology* 25, no. 3: 309–13.

Noonan, R. K., and D. Gibbs. 2009. "Empowerment Evaluation with Programs Designed to Prevent First-time Male Perpetration of Sexual Violence." *Health Promotion Practice* 10, no. 1: 5S–10S.

Noonan, R. K., J. G. Emshoff, A. Mooss, M. Armstrong, J. Weinberg, and B. Ball. 2009. "Adoption, Adaption, and Fidelity of Implementation of Sexual Assault Prevention Programs." *Health Promotion Practice* 10, no. 1: 59S–70S.

O'Connel, B. 1978. "From Service Delivery to Advocacy to Empowerment." *Social Casework* 59: 195–202.

Omi, M. 1980. "Review: The Declining Significance of Race by William Julius Wilson." *Insurgent Sociologist* 10, no. 2: 118–22.

Parsons, R. J. 2001. "Specific Practice Strategies for Empowerment-based Practice with Women: A Study of Two Groups." *AFFILIA* 16, no. 2: 159–79.

Patterson, J. T. 2000. *America's Struggle against Poverty in the Twentieth Century.* Cambridge: Harvard University Press.

Pearlin, L., and C. Schooler. 1978. "The Structure of Coping." *Journal of Health and Social Behavior* 19: 2–21.

Pernell, R. 1985. "Empowerment and Social Group Work." In *Innovations in Social Group Work: Feedback from Practice to Theory,* ed. M. Parenes, 107–17. New York: Haworth.

Perry, C. L., C. L. Williams, K. A. Komro, S. Veblen-Mortenson, H. Stigler, K. A. Munson, K. Farbakhsh, R. M. Jones, and J. L. Forster. 2002. "Project Northland: Long-term Outcomes of Community Action to Reduce Adolescent Alcohol Use." *Health Education Research* 17, no. 1: 117–32.

Peterson, K. J., and A. A. Lieberman. 2001. *Building on Women's Strengths: A Social Work Agenda for the Twenty-first Century.* 2nd ed. New York: Haworth Press.

Peterson, N. A., and J. Hughey. 2004. "Social Cohesion and Intrapersonal Empowerment: Gender as Moderator." *Health Education Research* 19, no. 5: 533–42.

Peterson, N. A., and R. J. Reid. 2003. "Paths to Psychological Empowerment in an Urban Community: Sense of Community and Citizen Participation in Substance Abuse Prevention Activities." *Journal of Community Psychology* 31, no. 1: 25–38.

Pettigrew, T. F. 1979. "Review: The Declining Significance of Race: Blacks and Changing American Institutions." *Michigan Law Review* 77: 917–24.

Piattelli-Palmarini, M. 1994. *Inevitable Illusions: How Mistakes of Reason Rule our Minds.* New York: John Wiley and Sons.

Pinderhughes, E. 1983. "Empowerment for Our Clients and for Ourselves." *Social Casework* 64: 331–38.

Piven, F. F., and R. A. Cloward. 1971. *Regulating the Poor: The Functions of Public Welfare.* New York: Vintage Press.

Putnam, R. 2001. *Bowling Alone: The Collapse and Revival of American Community.* New York: Touchstone Books.

Rappaport, J. 1981. "In Praise of Paradox: A Social Policy of Empowerment Over Prevention." *American Journal of Community Psychology* 9: 1–25.

Reamer, F. G. 1994. *The Foundations of Social Work Knowledge.* New York: Columbia University Press.

Resendez, M., R. Quist, and D. Matshazi. 2000. "A longitudinal analysis of family empowerment and client outcomes." *Journal of Child and Family Studies* 9, no. 4: 449–60.

Resnick, R. 1976. "Conscientization: An Indigenous Approach to International Social Work." *International Social Work* 19: 21–29.

Rieff, P. 1966. *The Triumph of the Therapeutic: Uses of Faith after Freud.* New York: Harper and Row.

Rodnitzky, J. L. 1999. *Feminist Phoenix: The Rise and Fall of a Feminist Counterculture.* Westport, CT: Praeger.

Rogers, E. M. 2003. *Diffusion of Innovations.* New York: Free Press.

Rose, S., and B. Black. 1985. *Advocacy and Empowerment: Mental Health Care in the Community.* Boston, MA: Routledge & Kegan Paul.

Sakamoto, A., and J. M. Tzeng. 1999. "A Fifty-year Perspective on the Declining Significance of Race in the Occupational Attainment of White and Black Men." *Sociological Perspectives* 42, no. 2: 157–79.

Saleebey, D. 1996. "The Strengths Perspective in Social Work Practice: Extensions and Cautions." *Social Work* 41, no. 3: 296–305.

Sarri, R., and V. du Rivage. 1985. *Strategies for Self Help and Empowerment of Working Low-income Women Who are Heads of Families.* Unpublished manuscript, University of Michigan, School of Social Work, Ann Arbor.

Schechter, S., S. Szymanski, M. Cahill. 1985. *Violence against Women: A Curriculum for Empowerment (Facilitator's Manual).* New York: Women's Education Institute.

Schraad-Tischler, D. 2011. *Social Justice in the OECD- How do the Member States Compare?* http://www.bertelsmann-stiftung.de/ (last accessed date 12/15/11)

Seabury, B. A., B. H. Seabury, and C. D. Gravin. 2011. *Foundations of Interpersonal Practice in Social Work.* Thousand Oaks, CA: Sage Publications.

Secret, M., A. Jordan, and J. Ford. 1999. "Empowerment Evaluation as a Social Work Strategy." *Health & Social Work* 24, no. 2: 120–27.

Shapiro, J. 1984. "Commitment to Disenfranchised Clients." In *Handbook of Clinical Social Work,* ed. A. Rosenblatt and D. Waldfogel, 888–903. San Francisco, CA: Jossey-Bass.

Sheafor, W. W., and C. R. Horejsi. 2003. *Techniques and Guidelines for Social Work Practice.* New York: Allyn and Bacon.

Sherman, W., and S. Wenocur. 1983. "Empowering Public Welfare Workers through Mutual Support." *Social Work* 28: 375–79.

Shils, E. 1965. "Charisma, Order, and Status." *American Sociological Review* 30, no. 2: 199–213.

———. 1982. "Knowledge and Sociology of Knowledge." *Knowledge: Creation, Diffusion, Utilization* 4, no. 1: 7–32.

Shreve, A. 1989. *Women Together, Women Alone.* New York: Viking.

Shulman, L. 2012. *The Skills of Helping Individuals, Families, Groups and Communities.* Belmont, CA: Brooks/Cole.

Shulman, S. 1981. "Race, Class, and Occupational Stratification: A Critique of William J. Wilson's the Declining Significance of Race." *Review of Radical Political Economics* 13, no. 21: 21–31.

Silver, R., and C. Wortman. 1980. "Coping with Undesirable Life Events." In *Human Helplessness: Theory and Application*, ed. J. Garber and M. Seligman, 279–375. New York: Academic Press.

Simmons, C., and R. Parsons. 1983a. "Developing Internality and Perceived Competence: The Empowerment of Adolescent Girls." *Adolescence* 18: 917–22.

———. 1983b. "Empowerment for Role Alternatives in Adolescence. *Adolescence* 18: 193–200.

Simon, B. L. 1994. *The Empowerment Tradition in American Social Work: A History.* New York: Columbia University Press.

Smail, D. 2005. *Power, Interest and Psychology.* Ross-on-Wye, UK: PCCS Books.

Solomon, B. 1976. *Black Empowerment.* New York: Columbia University Press.

———. 1982. "Empowering Women: A Matter of Values." In *Women, Power, and Change*, ed. A. Weick and S. Vandiver, 206–14. Silver Spring, MD: National Association of Social Workers.

Stein, L. I., and M. A. Test. 1980. "Alternatives to Mental Hospital Treatment." *Archives of General Psychiatry* 37: 392–412.

Stoesz, D., H. Karger, and T. Carillo. 2010. *A Dream Deferred: How Social Work Education Lost Its Way and What Can Be Done.* New Brunswick, NJ: Aldine Transaction.

Sundquist, J. L. 1978. "Review of the Declining Significance of Race: Blacks and Changing American Institutions." *Political Science Quarterly* 93, no. 3: 521–22.

Swigert V. L., and R. A. Farrell. 1977. "Normal Homicides and Law." *American Sociological Review* 42, no. 1: 16–32.

Tang, T., M. Funnell, M. Brown, and J. Kurlander. 2009. "Self-management support in 'real world' settings: an empowerment-based intervention." *Patient Education Counsel* 79, no. 2: 178–84.

Thoits, P. 1983. "Dimensions of Life Events that Influence Psychological Distress: An Evaluation and Synthesis of Literature." In *Psychosocial Stress: Trends in Theory and Research*, ed. H. Kaplan. New York: Academic Press. 212–37.

Thomas, M. E. 1993. "Race, Class, and Personal Income: An Empirical Test of the Declining Significance of Race Thesis, 1968-1988." *Social Problems* 40, no. 3: 328–42.

Throop, E. A. 2009. *Psychotherapy, American Culture, and Social Policy: Immoral Individualism.* New York: Palgrave Macmillan.

Trice, H. M. and J. M. Beyer. 1984. "Studying Organizational Cultures through Rites and Ceremonies." *Academy of Management Review* 9, no. 4: 653–69.

Turner, V. 1969. *The Ritual Process; Structure and Anti-Structure.* Ithaca, NY: Cornell University Press.

United States Department of Housing and Urban Development. *The 2010 Annual Homeless Assessment Report to Congress*. http://www.hudhre.info/documents/2010HomelessAssessmentReport.pdf (last accessed date 12/15/11).

———. *The 2009 Annual Homeless Assessment Report to Congress*. http://www.hudhre.info/documents/5thHomelessAssessmentReport.pdf (last accessed date 12/15/11).

———. *The 2008 Annual Homeless Assessment Report to Congress*. http://www.hudhre.info/documents/4thHomelessAssessmentReport.pdf (last accessed date 12/15/11).

———. *The 2007 Annual Homeless Assessment Report to Congress*. http://www.hud.gov/local/ms/news/pr2007-02-28.cfm (last accessed date 12/15/11).

———. *The 2005 Annual Homeless Assessment Report to Congress*, http://www.hud.gov/offices/cpd/homeless/hmis/strategy/reporttocongress2006.pdf (last accessed date 12/15/11).

United States House. 2008. "Committee on Ways and Means." *Overview of Entitlement Programs: Background Material and Data on the Programs within the Jurisdiction of the Committee on Ways and Means*. Washington, DC: US House of Representatives.

Van Den Bergh, N. 1995. *Feminist Practice in the 21st Century*. Washington, DC: NASW Press.

Van Den Bergh, N., and L. Cooper, L. eds. 1986. *Feminist Visions for Social Work*. Silver Springs, MD: National Association of Social Workers.

Van Gennep, A. 1960. *The Rites of Passage*. London: Routledge.

Wagenaar, A. C., J. P. Gehan, R. Jones-Webb, T. L. Toomey, and J. L. Forster. 1999. "Communities Mobilizing for Change on Alcohol: Lessons and Results from a 15-community Randomized Trial." *Journal of Community Psychology* 27, no. 3: 315–26.

Walker, K. 2007. "Youth Empowerment Evaluation: Learning Voice." *American Journal of Evaluation* 28, no. 3: 321–26.

Wandersman, A. P. Florin. 2003. "Community Interventions and Effective Prevention." *American Psychologist* 58, no. 6/7: 441–48.

Wapshott, N. 2011. *Keynes/Hayek: The Clash that Defined Modern Economics*. New York: Norton.

Waxman, C. I. 1977. *The Stigma of Poverty: A Critique of Poverty Theories and Policies*. New York: Pergamon Press.

Westinghouse Learning Corporation. 1969. *The Impact of Head Start: An Evaluation of the Effects of Head Start on Children's Cognitive and Affective Development*. Washington, DC: Clearinghouse for Federal Scientific and Technical Assistance.

Williams, J. 2006. *Enough*. New York: Crown Publishers.

Wilson, J. 1987. "Women and Poverty: A Demographic Overview." *Women and Health* 12: 21–40.

Wilson, W. J. 1978. *The Declining Significance of Race: Blacks and Changing American Institutions*. Chicago, IL: The University of Chicago Press.

Zambrana, R. 1987. "A Research Agenda on Issues Affecting Poor and Minority Women: A Model for Understanding their Health Needs." *Women and Health* 12: 137–60.

Zastrow, C. 2004. *An Introduction to Social Work and Social Welfare*. Belmont, CA: Brooks/Cole.

Zeece, P. D. and A. Wang. 1998. "Effects of the family empowerment and transitioning program on child and family outcomes." *Child Study Journal* 28, no. 3: 161–78.

Zeldin, S. 2004. "Preventing Youth Violence through the Promotion of Community Engagement and Membership." *Journal of Community Psychology* 32, no. 5: 623–41.

Zilbergeld, B. 1983. *The Shrinking of America: Myths of Psychological Change.* Boston, MA: Little, Brown.

Index

Abcedarian, 45
Adult Education Project, 18. *See* Friere, Paulo
Affirmative action, 24
African National Congress, 17
Allen-Meares, Paula, 63
Andrews, Ariene, 59
Angelique, Holly, 62
Angell, Marcia, 43

Ball, Barbara, 59
Beck, Judith, 54
Bellamy, Chyrell, 62
Bentley, 65
Berkeley, Kathleen, 35
Berkowitz, Bill, 50
Bertelsmann, 4
Bickman, Leonard, 47
Bohem, Amnon, 62
Bolivar, Simon, 35, 57
Boydell, Katherine, 62
Brenner, Johanna, 37
Bricker-Jenkins, Mary, 55
Broughten, 62
Budweiser, 10. *See also* Ceremony
Burghardt, Steve, 55
Burtless, Gary, 30

Carr, Sommerson, 62
Castro, Fidel, 18, 35
Ceremonial role, ix–x, 6, 9, 60, 76
Ceremonial, 2, 8–12, 14, 54, 60–61, 67, 76, 78, 86
  Function, 10, 12, 14, 54, 61, 67
Ceremonies, xi, 7–9, 11–13, 36, 77
Ceremony, 7, 9–14, 21, 49, 88
Chadiha, Letha, 27
Chaiklin, Harris, 34, 36, 56

Chan, Cecilia, 47
Chronister, Krista, 62
Cognitive behavioral therapy, 54
Cohen, Marcia, 35
Combs, Gene, 12
Community action, 49–50
Conscientization, 19, 35, 49, 54–55, 58
Consciousness raising, 20, 31, 35, 40–42, 52, 54–55, 71, 100–101
Consensus organizing, 49, 51–52
Conservative, 5, 24, 70, 86
Coontz, Stephanie, 40
Coppola, Francis, 29
Cosby, Bill, 65
Coser, Lewis, 22
Cox, Carole, 26–27

David Hume, ix
Davis, Angela, 40
De Madres a Madres, 37–38
Democratic populism, x, 2, 74, 84, 86–89
Democratic progressivism, x, 74, 84, 86–87
Denby, Ramona, 23
Diffusion theory, 50
Diversi, Marcelo, 62
Domina, Lynn, 12
Dubois, William, 30
Duflo, Esther, 65
Dunlap, Katherine, 47

Echols, Alice, 36
Economic crisis, 5
Economic mobility, 3–4, 36
Edwards, Harry, 65
Effectiveness, x, 21, 24, 26, 29, 43
Ego psychology, 27. *See* Psychotherapy

For Product Safety Concerns and Information please contact our EU representative GPSR@taylorandfrancis.com Taylor & Francis Verlag GmbH, Kaufingerstraße 24, 80331 München, Germany

Batch number: 08153776

Printed by Printforce, the Netherlands